Designed by Philip Clucas
Produced by Ted Smart and
   David Gibbon

CLB1958
© 1987 Colour Library Books Ltd.,
   Guildford, Surrey, England.
Printed and bound in Barcelona, Spain
   by Cronion, S.A.
All rights reserved.
Published 1987 by Crescent Books .
Distributed by Crown Publishers, Inc.
ISBN 0 517 65105 X
h g f e d c b a

THE WORLD OF
PRO FOOTBALL

TEXT BY
PAUL FICHTENBAUM

PHOTOGRAPHED BY
JOHN W. McDONOUGH

CRESCENT BOOKS
NEW YORK

Contents

Photographer's Dedication
To Mitz and Patrick, my appreciation and love.

Author's Dedication
To Mona, who taught me how to take the ball
and run with it.

SUPER BOWL

You might say that the New York Giants and Denver Broncos swept into Super Bowl XXI on completely different notes.

The Giants, champions of the National Football Conference, were simply overwhelming. They finished the regular season with a 14-2 mark, capturing the East Division (their first divisional championship in 23 years) by stringing nine straight victories after a midseason loss to Seattle. The Giants defense, the heart and soul of the team, allowed only 236 points in the regular campaign, second to the Bears. The offense, which started slowly due to Joe Morris' training camp holdout, showed that it could put points on the board quickly, with quarterback Phil Simms hitting the big play seemingly whenever the Giants needed it. The team as a whole was on a roll.

But the regular season was just a warmup for the playoffs. Since the first Super Bowl in 1967, never has a team had a more impressive, more dominating playoff than the Giants.

The San Francisco 49ers were the first team to feel the wrath of the Giants as the New Yorkers crushed the Niners 49-3, the most lopsided playoff game in years. Not only did the Giants embarrass the Niners, but they also pummelled them physically. In the second-quarter, nose tackle Jim Burt sent 49er quarterback Joe

Montana to the hospital with a vicious hit. And after Montana was gone so were San Francisco's chances.

Next was the NFC Championship game against the Washington Redskins. After defeating Washington twice in the regular season, the Giants skinned the Skins easily at the Meadowlands, 17-0. The New York defense completely suffocated the Redskin offense, and made Washington quarterback Jay Schroeder run for his life all afternoon. There was no question that the Giants were a Super team.

The Broncos, on the other hand, were fortunate to be playing for the big prize. They began the season looking like a Super Bowl team, winning their first six games and jumping to an early lead in the American Football Conference West Division. After that, though, the Broncos played under .500, yet still won their division.

The strength of this Denver team was the defense and its big-play quarterback John Elway. After two frustrating seasons in which Elway did not develop into the dominating signalcaller everybody anticipated, the Stanford grad put it all together and Denver's offense lived off the pass. There was never a question about the defense, though. Led by Pro Bowlers Rulon Jones and Karl Mecklenburg, the Broncos could always count on a solid effort.

And those two intangibles held up in the playoffs. Against the New England Patriots, Denver squeaked by, 24-20 with the finishing touches supplied by a safety. In the championship game the Browns were a stiffer challenge. The AFC's best team in the regular season led the Broncos 20-16 late in the game, until a miracle last-minute drive by Elway catapulted Denver to the Super Bowl. Many people, especially in Cleveland, felt Denver didn't belong in the big game.

And the oddsmakers agreed. The NFC champs were posted as eight-point favorites over the Broncos, a spread the Giants felt was ridiculously high. After all, this was the same Denver team that the Giants beat 19-16 in the regular season on a field goal with only six seconds left. The same team that Giants could not score an offensive touchdown against (their only TD in that game was an interception return by defensive end George Martin).

"We were lucky to come out of that game with a win," admitted Giants offensive tackle Karl Nelson.

"We only beat them by three points in New York, a home game," said Giants coach Bill Parcells. "The teams are much closer than that. Everybody knows that. I think it just happens to be a product of the way we've played in the last couple of weeks."

The Broncos, on the other hand, loved the fact that they were such underdogs. They knew they had outplayed the Giants in the regular season game, outgaining them in total yardage 405-262. The only difference was in turnovers, where Denver coughed up the ball four times.

"People thinking we're not very good is not new," said Denver's veteran linebacker Tom Jackson, who played for Denver in Super Bowl XI, the Broncos' only other trip to the Super Bowl. "But I think this: I think the Giants thought they were going to lose to us with two minutes left in that game in November. Well, we're excited about playing them again."

But the Giants were just as excited. "The bomb is ticking inside all of us," said New York guard Chris Godfrey.

"Every situp, every sprint all of us has ever gone through, everything we've done athletically, has been for this," said Giants wide receiver Phil McConkey. "Think of the time we've spent in the gyms, on fields, in locker

New York Giants quarterback Phil Simms (facing page) proved his worth in the Super Bowl against the Denver Broncos. The eighth-year signalcaller from Morehead State, who has been plagued by injuries early in his career, completed a Super Bowl record 22 of 25 passes for 268 yards and three touchdowns.

rooms. It's for this. Everybody in life wants to do something great. We're on the threshold of it right now."

And how. The performance of the Giants in Super Bowl XXI was simply super. Before a crowd of 101,063 in the Rose Bowl, the New Yorkers dismantled the Broncos piece by

New York quarterback Phil Simms must have been thinking the same thing. Simms, who had been booed much of his career as a Giant, had a remarkable day, completing 22 of 25 passes for 268 yards. He threw three touchdowns – six-yard scoring strikes to Zeke Mowatt and Phil McConkey

and a 13-yard TD toss to Mark Bavaro – and was not intercepted. In the process, Simms broke the Super Bowl record for completion percentage set by Ken Anderson (73.5 percent) with his 88 percent accuracy. His 10 straight completions was also a Super Bowl record. His heroics won him the

piece, scoring the first 24 points in the second half to crush Denver 39-20.

"I'm getting my Super Bowl ring," said Giants linebacker Lawrence Taylor, "and I'm going to sport it all over Williamsburg (Va., his home town). As long as I have that Super Bowl ring, that's one thing they can't take away from me. They can say what they want about the Giants and all those (bad) years, but we're the best team in the world. That's the most important thing for me. For one year, we're the best in the world."

"My guys were just magnificent," said Giants coach Bill Parcells. "This is a great thrill for me. I figure I am one of the luckiest guys in the world. Why God blessed me in this way, I don't know."

Super Bowl XXI was a painful experience for Denver Broncos' place kicker Rich Karlis. The barefooted booter (above) missed two short field goal attempts in the first half of the game, giving the Giants the momentum for the second half. Phil McConkey (facing page) enjoyed the Super Bowl as much as any Giants' player. The former pilot from the Navy caught a third-quarter touchdown pass from Phil Simms that bounced off the hands of New York tight end Mark Bavaro.

Sport Magazine MVP trophy – unanimously.

"I still have a hard time believing what I did," Simms said afterwards. "To play that good of a game in a game of this magnitude is just unbelievable."

"I didn't throw one ball today when I said, 'Damn, I want that one back.' They showed no respect for us throwing the ball. That's why we came out throwing."

The Giants game plan certainly did take the Broncos by surprise. "They surprised us right off the way they came out throwing," said Denver nose tackle Ken Kragen. "They went against the tendencies they showed us in their last few games. We picked that up right away, but they caught us by surprise."

"You've got to give credit to their offense," said Denver quarterback John Elway. "They controlled the ball. The best defense is a great offense. Simms had a great day. Anytime you throw three touchdowns, I'm sure it's a dream come true for him."

But Simms and the offense wasn't the only reason the Broncos had a nightmare of a time in Pasadena. The Giants defense, the unit which carried New York through most of the season, stood tall when it counted, although Elway had a fine day at the Broncos' helm.

The 6-3 quarterback completed 22 of 37 passes for 304 yards. He threw one TD pass and also tossed an interception. Elway was able to scramble for a team-leading 27 yards on the ground and accounted for 305 of the Broncos' 372 net yards.

"I guess I never feel any fulfillment when we lose," Elway said. "But I came out of this game saying I did everything I could. I wasn't uptight. I was disappointed but not embarrassed."

So were the rest of the Broncos. Especially after the quick start that almost made the oddsmakers eat their points.

On Denver's first possession, Elway masterfully directed his team down the field against the seemingly invincible Giants defense. The first play from scrimmage was just what the Giants feared most as Elway scampered out of the pocket for a 10-yard gain.

"Getting (Washington quarterback Jay) Schroeder out of the pocket (in the NFC Conference Championship game) was a plus for us," said Giants nose tackle Jim Burt. "Getting Elway out of the pocket is a minus for us."

Two plays later Elway hit wide receiver Mark Jackson for a 24-yard gain, giving Denver the ball on the Giants 39-yard line. The New Yorkers were able to hold Denver, but the Broncos cashed in on a long 48-yard field goal by Rich Karlis for a 3-0 advantage.

The New York Giants defense put the clamps on the Orange Crush of Denver. Here, Jim Burt and Carl Banks wrestle a Bronco to the turf.

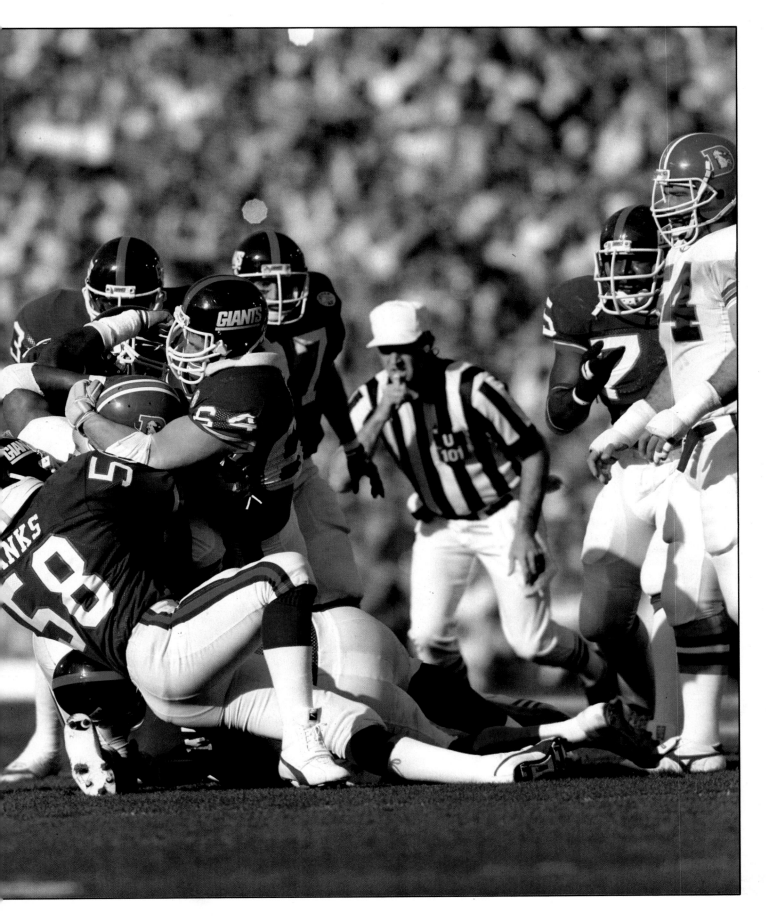

That lead didn't last long as Simms quickly led the Giants on a brilliant drive. Simms took the team 78 yards in only nine plays, most of that through the air, culminating in a six-yard TD pass to reserve tight end Zeke Mowatt. On the drive, Simms hit on six of six passes for 69 yards as the Giants took the lead 7-3.

Next it was Elway's turn to riddle the New York defense. Starting at the Giants 42-yard line, Elway hit on passes to Sammy Winder (14 yards) Orson Mobley (11 yards) and Winder (nine yards) again. Then Giants linebacker Harry Carson creamed Winder when the running back was out of bounds, resulting in a penalty. When Lawrence Taylor disputed the call by throwing the penalty flag, the Broncos had first and goal at the six. Two plays later, Elway executed a perfect quarterback draw, rushing for a four-yard TD and a 10-7 Denver lead.

The first half was quickly becoming a duel between Simms and Elway as the two star quarterbacks hit on 20 of their first 23 pass attempts. For Denver, Elway's hot hand in the passing department was needed; the Broncos' inability at running the football was becoming clear. But not any clearer than on the next series, when Denver could easily have turned the game in their favor.

Once again Elway directed his team into Giants territory, this time bringing Denver to the New York one-yard line with first and goal. A touchdown would give Denver a commanding 17-7 lead, but the Giants defense showed why it was one of the NFL's best.

On first down, Elway tried to sweep right but was brought down by Lawrence Taylor for a loss of one. On second down, running back Gerald Willhite was tackled for a yard loss by Carson and Eric Dorsey. Then on third down, Winder attempted a sweep and linebackers Carson and Carl Banks brought him down for another loss, this time two yards. The Giants goal-line stand was reminiscent of the great defensive stand by San Francisco in Super Bowl XVI against Cincinnati, a series of downs that proved to be the turning point in that game – and also in this one.

"They were all stacked inside," said Elway of the Giants defense on the third down play. "We thought we

John Elway (above) barks signals, but can't take the bite out of the Giants defense. Little Joe Morris (facing page, top) was provided with huge holes and ran through the Denver defense all day. Giants tight end Mark Bavaro (bottom right) did not say much to the media in Super Bowl week, but his actions on the field are enough to get the Broncos' attention.

could run outside. We missed a block and they got quick penetration by the cornerback from the outside. As soon as he got in the play was over."

"We were moving extremely well. We had a lot of momentum," said Denver receiver Steve Watson. "If we got up 17-7, I felt we could've blown it wide open. We could have forced them to play a scrambling type of defense."

Unfortunately for the Broncos, they couldn't put any points on the board. Denver place kicker Rich Karlis came in on fourth down to attempt a chip shot – 23 yards – and give Denver a 13-7 lead. But Karlis pushed the ball wide right and the momentum swung heavily to the Giants.

"We lost some air out of our balloon," said Watson. "It bolsters the confidence of the defense and it

brings the offense off the field shaking their heads and wondering why we got no points."

But that missed kick by Karlis wasn't the only one. With only seconds left in the first half, Karlis missed again – this time from 34 yards – and instead of leaving the field with 16 points in the half, the Broncos settled for only 10.

"It was definitely the deciding factor in the game," said a downcast Karlis about his failed opportunities. "Those misses were real significant. They definitely shifted the momentum. I really feel I let them back in the game."

Before the half was over the Giants edged even closer to the Broncos. On the ensuing series after the first missed field goal, defensive end Leonard Marshall sacked Elway for a two yard loss to the Denver 13. The following play, Elway hit tight end Clarence Kay for a 13-yard reception only to have one of the officials rule that the pass was trapped. Replays from the television booth seemed to indicate that Kay did, indeed, make a clean catch. Then, on third and 12, George Martin trapped Elway two yards inside the end zone for a Giants safety. With only 2:46 left in the half, the Giants cut the deficit to 10-9.

New York knew they were lucky only to trail by a point after the first half and the Giants showed their gratitude by blowing the game open in the third quarter. On their initial drive, the Giants were stalled on the Denver 46 with a fourth down when coach Bill Parcells reached into his bag of tricks. With one yard to go for the first down, backup quarterback Jeff Rutledge lined up as the upback in punt formation only to walk under the center, take the snap and rush for a first down.

Simms and the offense capitalized on that bit of trickery as the blond quarterback hit on consecutive passes to Joe Morris (12 yards) and Lee Rouson (23 yards) before connecting with Mark Bavaro for a 13-yard scoring pass. The Giants led 16-10 and it was downhill from there for Denver.

The Broncos' ground game continued to fail – they managed 14 yards in 12 carries in the first half – and Denver were forced to lean too heavily on Elway for a miracle. But the Giants defenders, forgetting about

As expected, the Giants were able to penetrate the Denver offensive line and flush John Elway out of the pocket during the Super Bowl. Unfortunately for New York, Elway proved to be very elusive as Lawrence Taylor (facing page, top) and Carl Banks (facing page, bottom) just can't get a handle on the Broncos' star quarterback. Reserve offensive tackle William Roberts (above) celebrates the New York win like he danced in the Giants' video – uninhibited.

the run, chased Elway all over the field, taking his receivers out of the game. Three plays and out for the Broncos offense.

Phil McConkey fielded the Denver punt and returned it 25 yards to the Bronco 36-yard line. Simms drove the team down, but couldn't punch it in the end zone, although Raul Allegre booted a 21-yard field goal for a 19-10 advantage. The rout was beginning to take shape.

Once again the Giants defense shut down Elway, allowing Simms and the offense to trot back onto the field. And once again Parcells' trickery paid off. On second down and six from the Denver 45, Simms handed off to Morris who then pitched back to Simms on a flea flicker. McConkey

raced downfield and Simms hit him with a spiral at the five before Mark Haynes knocked the Navy receiver out of bounds at the one-yard line. Morris finished the drive by sweeping untouched into the end zone. The third quarter ended with the Giants holding a 26-10 lead. The rout was officially on.

It continued in the final period. On the second play, New York cornerback Elvis Patterson intercepted an Elway pass. Everything was going the Giants' way now and that was demonstrated on the Giants drive.

Simms, trying to put the game out of reach, fired a bullet to Bavaro in the end zone and the big tight end bobbled the ball amidst a bunch of Denver defensive backs. Instead of falling into the waiting hands of a Bronco, the ball fell right into the lap of McConkey for six more points. The PAT by Allegre was good and the rout was finished.

"The story of my career is working my rear end off to get everything," said McConkey. "That play, and this game, reflected that ethic perfectly."

Just for good measure the Giants scored one more time before Denver closed the gap for a final score of 39-20. It wasn't that close.

The Giants and their fans waited 31 years for that championship and, before the game was even officially over, New York began to celebrate. Harry Carson traded his uniform for a security guard's and doused Bill Parcells with the traditional bucket of Gatorade. Many players followed Carson's lead, disrobing, waving towels and leading the cheers.

"I knew it was over for a long time," said Lawrence Taylor. "When I saw McConkey catch that tipped pass for a touchdown, then I really knew we couldn't be beaten."

"There are no words that can truly describe how I feel," said long-suffering Giants linebacker Harry Carson. "This morning I was thinking about when I was young and I watched the Super Bowl I and my heroes were Willie Davis and Buck Buchanan. I had T-shirts and I'd put their numbers on them. I was thinking how there might be kids who'll put 53, my number, on T-shirts just like I did. It's an experience just being here. To win it, it's very gratifying."

Forty-four other Giants will attest to that.

AFC CHAMPIONSHIP

The day the Denver Broncos defeated the Cleveland Browns in the American Football Conference Championship game could have been named two ways. The first would be called John Elway day. That, of course, is the moniker the Broncos would give.

Across the line of scrimmage it could have been called Pay Back day, for the Browns were paid in the exact way they paid the Jets a week earlier in the AFC divisional playoffs; with a pink slip. A last-minute drive catapulted the game into overtime and one team eventually found its way onto the unemployment line for the rest of the campaign.

This time, though, it was the Browns who were singing the blues, green with envy at the thought of the Orange Crush going to the Rose Bowl. And as the Broncos stormed onto the field at frozen Cleveland Municipal Stadium to celebrate their unlikely 23-20 victory, one man stood as the reason for victory – Denver quarterback John Elway.

It has not been an easy ride to the top for Elway, even though he was the number one player selected in the 1984 NFL draft. Sure he was paid handsomely for that honor, but just as sure the people writing the paychecks and purchasing the tickets wanted a winner – immediately. And while he had been progressing steadily, he really never arrived – until that drive which began at his own two-yard line with 5:32 remaining and the Broncos down by seven points.

"Hey, potential is a big word, a tough word to get rid of," said the 26-year-old Elway. "But if we win the next game (the Super Bowl), then maybe I can do it."

"He is extremely competitive and it really hurts him to hear the criticism,"

said Elway's coach Dan Reeves, who admits that he expected too much from Elway his first two seasons. "I could see the determination in his eyes today like I've never seen before. He wanted to play so badly and I think he proved to a lot of people that he's come a long way.

"You can't believe the pressure John has been under since he joined the team. His buildup was so big that people expected every pass he threw to go for a touchdown.

"He's had his ups and downs, but he's a tough person. And I think the toughness that he demonstrated in the offseason led to what you saw him do against Cleveland."

What he did against Cleveland was simply rally his team from a desperate situation. With the score tied at 13, Cleveland's own comeback kid, Bernie Kosar, led his club on a 52-yard three play drive. After two rushing plays, Koson went to the air, hitting wide receiver Brian Brennan with a 48-yard touchdown and a 20-13 lead. And after the kickoff was mishandled by Denver's Ken Bell and downed at the two-yard line, Elway needed 98 yards just to get Denver tied. A near impossible situation for a veteran quarterback, let alone a youngster. Plus with the freezing wind and icy conditions, the game was certainly one for the defenses.

Five minutes, thirty two seconds. Ninety eight yards. Elway probably could barely see the other end zone. But he knew he had to get there.

"In the huddle after that kickoff to the two he smiled. I couldn't believe it," remembered Broncos receiver Steve Watson. "He said, 'If you work hard, good things are going to happen.' And then he smiled again."

"As a quarterback, you have to remain calm," said Elway of his actions

on the last drive. "You can't be like a linebacker and go a hundred miles an hour."

"For us, it was 98 yards to the Super Bowl," said rookie receiver Mark Jackson. "But in the face of adversity, true champions are born."

And how. Elway began the drive with a five yard pass to running back Sam Winder, then handed off to Winder consecutively for the first down. Eighty eight yards to go. And the clock is ticking.

Three yards on a rush then Elway sprints out of the backfield for 11 more and a first down at the 26. Seventy four yards to go. Tick, tick, tick. On first down Elway hits Steve Sewell with a flare and the running back rambles to the Denver 48. Fifty two yards to go. Another first down, another first down pass. This time to Watson for 12 yards. Forty yards to go. Tick, tick, tick. Two minutes on the clock.

"The onus on stopping him (Elway) rests with out secondary," said Browns' coach Marty Schottenheimer. "If I tell our defensive linemen to try to contain him, they'll stand around like three or four traffic cops."

Steve Sewell of the Broncos and Tracy Rockins of the Browns (facing page, top) tangle after the Denver running back pulls down a pass. John Elway (facing page, bottom) led the Broncos into the Super Bowl with a masterful performance, bringing Denver back from a touchdown deficit with less than six minutes to play. Browns quarterback Bernie Kosar (overleaf) isn't fleet, but here he outruns two Denver linemen.

After a first-down incompletion, the linemen didn't stand around like traffic cops, sacking Elway for an 18-yard loss back to the Denver 48. Time out, Broncos.

"When I went over to the sideline, he (coach Reeves) told me to try to go for only half of what we needed because we still had two plays to get the 18 yards (for the first down)," said Elway. "We called a 'release 66 pass, with Orson Mobley (the tight end) as the primary receiver, about 10 yards over the middle. But as we lined up, I saw that their strong safety (Ray Ellis) was playing very, very deep and that we had a good chance to go for the whole 18 yards. So, instead of looking for Mobley, I looked for Jackson."

And he found him. Twenty yards downfield for a Denver first down at the 28. Twenty eight yards left, 1:19 on the clock. Tick, tick. On the next play Elway got half of what he needed with a 14-yard completion to Sewell. He followed that with a nine yard scramble. Five yards and 42 seconds to go. The following play brought the tying touchdown as Elway connected with Jackson in the end zone. No yards to go, 23 ticks to spare.

"I thought their cornerback (Hanford Dixon) would bump Jackson at the line of scrimmage," Elway said. "But when he didn't, it was Mark against the safety one on one. No problem."

Maybe that drive, but certainly not every one before that.

Cleveland got onto the board first on a superbly executed drive by Kosar. The former University of Miami product led the Browns 86 yards in 14 plays, culminating with a six-yard scoring pass to Herman Fontenot. The Broncos answered back early in the second quarter on a 19-yard field goal by Rich Karlis to cut the deficit to 7-3. Less than two minutes later, Denver took the lead as Gerald Willhite bulled in from the one for a 10-7 Broncos advantage. The Browns knotted it 20 seconds before halftime on a 29-yard field goal by Mark Moseley.

The second half was a similar chess match. Denver scored first on a 26-yard field goal by Karlis, but Cleveland answered with a Moseley field goal (24 yards) and Kosar's 48-yard strike to Brennan. Cleveland led, 20-13, before Elway stamped himself a star with his 98-yard march. But his long march just sent the game into overtime, where he again provided the heroics

Cleveland won the toss, but Kosar couldn't move his team against the tough Bronco defense. Elway took over at his 25-yard line and moved the team deftly. He hit Mobley for 22 yards and then lofted a spiral over cornerback Dixon's head for a 28-yard gain to Watson. Three rushing plays and the game was in the hands, or more precisely, on the foot, of Karlis.

"I tried to tell myself it was just another kick," said the bare-footed Karlis. "I tried to psych myself by saying, 'Hey, if I miss it, I'll get another chance.'

"When I got out to my kicking spot, I knew there was a lot of sand on the field so I tried to brush some of it away, but I only succeeded in digging a hole. Finally, I said, 'To heck with it. Just kick the ball'

"And I pulled it. All afternoon I was right down the middle. But with the Super Bowl on the line, I pulled it."

But not enough to miss. "After I saw it go through I got out of the way fast," Karlis recalled. "I was afraid my teammates would smother me and it doesn't take much to smother a 170-pounder."

If his teammates should smother anybody, they should have smothered Elway. "You saw one of the greatest competitors in the business today," agreed Karlis.

Elway saw it a different way. "You know how you'll think the night before about how you'd like to do great things in the game," Elway said afterward. "Well, this is the kind of game you dream about."

Not if you're a Brown. Then it's the kind of game you have a nightmare about.

Rich Karlis (3) and Gary Kubiak (8) have reason to celebrate (left) after the Broncos' place kicker booted a game-winning field goal against Cleveland to propel Denver to the Super Bowl.

NFC CHAMPIONSHIP

There would be no secrets, no trick plays in this one. Not with these two teams. When the Giants and Redskins strap on the pads, tape up the ankles and pull on the headgear, it's a guaranteed war.

During the regular season, the Giants won World War I, 27-20 in a memorable Monday night affair. World War II also went to the Giants, 24-14 in a game that virtually decided the NFC East Division winner. Nobody expected World War III to be any different.

After all, these two teams are very similar. Both have dominating rushing games, the Giants led by All Pro Joe Morris, who ran for 1,516 yards in the regular campaign. The Redskins rely on workhorse George Rogers, who joined Morris as a 1,000-yard rusher with 1,203 yards.

Both have big play quarterbacks. The Giants are blessed with Phil Simms, who hit for 3,487 yards passing and 21 touchdowns. The Skins counter with Jay Schroeder, the youngster with a rifle arm (he was the only quarterback beside Dan Marino to throw for more than 4,000 yards) and long-ball wide receivers in Art Monk and Gary Clark.

Both have good defenses. Well, not really. And that's where the difference is. The Redskins do have a good defense. The Giants, though, have a great defense. Bolstered by All Pro linemen Jim Burt and Leonard Marshall, All Pro linebackers Lawrence Taylor and Harry Carson, the Giants have the defense to dominate an opponent.

They proved that against the San Francisco 49ers a week earlier, when they crushed Bill Walsh's crew in a 49-3 win. Holding the Niners to three points is not exactly like holding the Indianapolis Colts to three points. No way. San Fran possess one of the finest quarterbacks in the game, Joe Montana. One of the finest all-around running backs in the game, Roger Craig. One of the finest wide receivers in the game, Jerry Rice. Together, the three helped the Niners rank as the third best offense in the NFL, averaging 23 points and 380 yards per contest.

All the Giants did was knock out Montana in the second quarter and help San Francisco attain a slew of negative records. The Giants defense was so good in that game, it would be hard for them to top that performance.

Or would it?

The 49ers did something that even the mighty Redskins couldn't in the NFC Championship game. Score a point. The Giants defense was the Atomic Bomb in World War II as the New Yorkers swamped the Skins 17-0 at the Meadowlands to make its first trip to the Super Bowl.

"I feel really great for the fans," said Carson, a veteran of the Giants' down years. "They've suffered for 23 years. Now I hope their suffering is over, because I'm tired of hearing about those 23 years of suffering."

"We were the pits for a lot of years," said George Martin, the Giants defensive end. "But now maybe we'll establish our own dynasty, so they'll have something else to talk about."

One thing the fans will talk about was the performance of the Giants defense in the champsionship game. New York held the high-powered Redskin offense to only 12 first downs and 190 net yards. Washington's ground game was held to a season-low 40 yards and Jay Schroeder, when he wasn't running for his life (he was sacked four times for a minus 45 yards), passed for 150 yards through the air. The key stat, in fact an unbelieveable stat, was Washington's inability to convert third-down situations. For the game, the Redskins were 0-14, almost a perfect performance by the Giants defense.

"Our defense didn't play a perfect game except in that department," said winning coach Bill Parcells. "When you hold a team in that department to 0-18 (including four unsuccessful fourth down tries by Washington), it's not perfect, it's a miracle. You get those three-downs-and-punt series, it's artistic."

The Giants were more than artistic; they were cerebral. With wind conditions inside Giants Stadium more conducive to a hurricane than a football game, the Giants won the toss and elected to kick off. Highly irregular, but also highly intelligent. Bill Parcells wanted his team's strongest unit, the defense, to have the advantage. If they could shut down the Redskins passing attack with the help of the wind, the Giants offense might have field position to put an early score on the board.

"I could see what was on Coach Parcells' mind," said Carson. "We had to go out there anyway, so why not let the defense go out there first."

"We knew they had to try to run the ball," said New York defensive coordinator Bill Belichick, "so we were prepared. We just go out and try to knock the guy's socks off. We don't want to interfere with our natural ability by giving them (the defense) too much to think about."

Joe Morris (facing page) received a lot of help from blocking back Maurice Carthon in 1986 and here is no different. The 5–7, 190-pound running back follows Carthon's lead block against Denver in Super Bowl XXI for another long gain.

little. You have to shorten your drop on a day like today."

Schroeder, who was dropped four times by the ferocious Giants defense, complained that the wind was the worst he ever played in. That excuse, however, didn't sit well with his mates.

"We got the ball for 30 minutes with the wind and 30 minutes against it, the same as them," said Washington safety Curtis Jordan. "We scored zero both ways. They turn the ball over on their 37 (Joe Morris had fumbled) at the end of the first half and we have the wind. What do we get out of it? Zero."

Exactly. And while the Redskins were fighting to remove the zero on the scoreboard, the Giants were adding to their side of the slate. In the second quarter, Simms orchestrated a fabulous drive against the wind, culminating in a one-yard TD plunge by Morris. At halftime the score read Giants 17, Washington 0. It also was the final score as the Giants sat on their lead in the second half. Simms passed the ball only twice in the second half, handing off to Morris most of the time instead of putting the ball in the swirling winds. With the dominating defense that the Giants possess, it was an easy victory.

"This was the first game that I felt we belonged," said Simms. "This was our game to win, on our field, in front of our fans and the other team had to come to us. I'm not surprised by what happened. We felt we should win."

And they did. Convincingly. Making World War III a quick and easy victory.

But his unit sure gave the Redskins much to think about. The first time Washington touched the ball it was three plays and out. The Skins couldn't run on the Giants and couldn't pass the ball on the wind. Punter Steve Cox could only manage a 23-yard kick into the teeth of the wind and the Giants had fabulous field position at the Washington 47. Six plays later, Raul Allegre booted a 47-yard field goal for a 3-0 Giants lead.

Washington's next possession was similar to its first. Three plays and bring on the punter. Cox again fought against the wind and lost. This time his punt traveled 27 yards. Giants' ball on the Redskin 38.

This time it took eight plays to score as Simms connected with Lionel Manuel on an 11-yard TD strike. Giants lead 10-0 in the first quarter. It was all but game, set and match.

"Cox is usually a super punter into the wind," said his opposite number, Giants punter Sean Landetta. "But today he told me he couldn't buy one. I think the wind was moving his drop a

A tradition continues. After each New York Giants' victory, linebacker Harry Carson dumps a jug of Gatorade on the head of coach Bill Parcells (left). Last season, Parcells was hit with 14 buckets in the regular season and three more in the playoffs. Giant defenders Elvis Patterson and Lawrence Taylor (facing page) congratulate themselves on another fine defensive performance. Taylor led the National Football League in sacks with 21.5 and once again proved he's the most dominating player in the game.

THE TEAMS

NFC EAST

New York Giants

There is no question that the Super Bowl champion New York Giants are the team to beat again this year, and for good reason. Not only did the Giants demolish the competition in the playoffs – beating San Francisco 49-3, Washington 17-0 and Denver 39-20 – but they got stronger in the offseason.

The only glaring weakness on these Giants is at receiver, where the incumbents – Lionel Manuel and Bobby Johnson – were less than consistent. Actually, Manuel was consistent – consistently injured – and Johnson didn't partake in New York's offseason weight training program. So all coach Bill Parcells did was choose Florida's outstanding wideout Mark Ingram with the first round selection in the draft, and Fresno State's Stephen "The Touchdown Maker" Baker in the third round.

In between those two picks, Parcells grabbed another blue-chip, Florida safety Adrian White, who is expected to bolster the Giants' defensive backfield. But there's really not much need on defense, not after the Giants' amazing performance in 1986.

The list of stars is seemingly endless: All Pros Lawrence Taylor, who led the NFL in sacks with 20½ and was named Most Valuable Player, nose tackle Jim Burt, defensive end Leonard Marshall and Taylor's partner at linebacker Harry Carson. But the fun doesn't stop there. Consider future Pro Bowler (he should have made it last year) Carl Banks, linebacker Gary Reasons, old-pro and big-play man George Martin and promising youngsters Erik Howard (nose tackle), John Washington (defensive end) and Pepper Martin (linebacker).

Quarterback Phil Simms emerged in a big way as a bonafide star in the Super Bowl, completing a record 22 of 25 throws for 288 yards. Joe Morris settled his contract problem just before the season and finished second in the NFL in rushing with 1,516 yards.

This is a team that is solid up and down the lineup. A repeat of last season would not be a surprise.

Washington Redskins

If it weren't for the Giants, the Washington Redskins would have been the best team in football. After all, they did finish with a 12-4 record (two of those losses were to the Giants), and they did crush the defending Super Bowl champion Chicago Bears, 27-14, in the divisional playoffs. The only thing that was between the Redskins and another Super Bowl appearance was, that's right, the Giants. The Redskins did get thumped by New York, 17-0, in the NFC Championship game, but don't count these 'Skins out this season.

They're a talented bunch and no one is more talented than quarterback Jay Schroeder. In only his first season as a starter, Schroeder not only made the Pro Bowl, but he shattered Hall-of-Famer Sonny Jurgenson's club record by throwing for 4,109 yards. He also tossed 22 touchdown passes and

The Giants defense was the second best unit in the league overall, finishing first against the run and ninth versus the pass, and the most outstanding section of the defense was the linebacking corps. Right: two of the unheralded backers – Carl Banks (58) and Gary Reasons (55) put the squeeze on Los Angeles Raiders running back Frank Hawkins.

Philadelphia Eagles

Poor Buddy Ryan. The former Chicago Bears defensive coordinator really put his foot in his mouth last season after he took over the head coaching position of the floundering Philadelphia Eagles. Not only did Ryan claim that he would turn around the franchise quickly, but he also predicted that the Eagles would make the playoffs. The Amazing Creskin he's not.

Tom Landry (right) had plenty of reason to turn his back on his Cowboys as Dallas posted an unCowboy-like 7-9 record in '86. George Rogers (facing page) anchored the Redskins to the ground, gaining over 1,000 yards. The head man of the Giants, Bill Parcells (below) called all the right shots.

The Eagles not only didn't make the playoffs, they didn't even finish with a .500 record. Philadelphia suffered through a 2-6 started and completed its first season under the volatile Ryan at 5-10-1. Not exactly championship bound, heh?

However, Ryan did do some good things. The first thing was to clean the Philly roster of players who didn't want to be there. By season's end, the Eagles had 20 new faces including 14 rookies, four of which made the all-rookie team. So despite the abysmal start, better things are expected in Ryan's second year.

"In most cases, the biggest jump in ability and performance that you see in NFL players is from the time they are rookies to the time they go into their sophomore year," says Ryan. We'll be watching.

The biggest problem on the Eagles last season was its offensive line. The line allowed an NFL-record 104 quarterback sacks, an amazing total considering the tremendous scrambling ability of quarterback Randall Cunningham. To help improve this unit, Ryan brought in Bill Walsh as the new offensive line coach. Despite its performance in '86, Ryan feels this unit will eventually come together.

We're very young," Ryan says, but we've got some good football players. They just need to improve on techniques and become tougher-type players. We're going to make sure they work harder."

One person Ryan doesn't have to push to work harder is defensive end Reggie White. The former USFL star became an NFL All Pro by terrorizing offensive tackles for 18 sacks. He has plenty of help on defense with middle linebacker Mike Reichenbach and outside man Alonzo Johnson, who will be entering his second season.

So far Buddy Ryan is not making any bold predictions about the performance of the 1987 Eagles. Is there any wonder why?

Dallas Cowboys

The Dallas Cowboys 7-9? That's got to be a typo, right? Wrong. For the first time in 22 seasons, the Dallas Cowboys suffered through a losing campaign and America's Team finds itself on the ropes trying to rebound.

"We were a losing team," says Cowboys coach Tom Landry, who has guided Dallas since its inception into the league 27 years ago. "We need help in a lot of places. Our success had given us late drafts for many years and it caught up with us."

And how. After a 6-2 start, the 'Boys lost seven of their remaining eight contests as Landry searched for the answers. One of the answers may be in youthful quarterback Steve Pelluer, who started the season as backup to Danny White, replaced the aging White when injuries ruined his season, and responded admirably. The three-year vet displayed skills reminiscent of Roger Staubach's, the former Cowboy and Hall of Famer. Pelluer threw for 2,727 yards, seven touchdowns and showed an uncanny ability to make things happen on the scramble.

"He is probably the most gifted quarterback we've had as far as mobility," says Landry of Pelluer. "Even Roger (Staubach) could never get out as quick and run as well as Pelluer. You watch film after film and it's amazing how they can get him bottled up and he'll just dip and slide and come out of there. If we can protect him, he can win for us."

To help him win, the Cowboys have a pair of Heisman Trophy winners in the backfield for the premier running combination in the league. With Tony Dorsett, the veteran tailback, and Herschel Walker, the powerful ex-USFLer, the Cowboys are set in the backfield. Last season Walker rushed for 737 yards and caught a club record 76 passes. It would not be surprising to see Walker rush and catch for over 2,000 total yards. Dorsett, though, had offseason surgery and his status is questionable. Even if Dorsett doesn't bounce back as quickly as hoped, Dallas will still be in good shape.

"Herschel might be the key to carrying us through the down time that every team faces after being on top so long," Landry admits. "(Herschel) is our ace in the hole."

And for the first time in 22 years, the Cowboys found themselves in a hole.

Herschel Walker proved to be a double threat for the Cowboys after he signed a contract following the demise of the USFL. Walker (right) rushed for 737 yards and caught 76 passes for 837 yards. The bite left the 'Boys in '86 as Dallas finished 23rd against the run, although John Elway (overleaf) wouldn't know it after being wrapped up by big John Dutton.

St. Louis Cardinals

Help! That's the operative word in St. Louis heading towards the 1987 season. The team that just three years ago was predicted to be headed for the Super Bowl, doesn't look like it could make it to the Cotton Bowl. Just listen to head coach Gene Stallings.

"We've got to have an outstanding running back. We've got to have an outstanding quarterback. We've got to have a leading touchdown catcher. We've got to have somebody who's going to get us

Cards pick) and acquiring several players or draft choices, St. Louis continued its ragged display on draft day. Who can forget last season's surprise (and disappointing, at least in St. Louis) fifth overall selection, Anthony Bell?

Why the Cards needed Stouffer anyway is a mystery. They seem to have given up on Neil Lomax, who was a Pro Bowl player in 1984. By the start of the 1987 season, the former Portland State product should be leading the Raiders (or Seahawks) if

The defensive line will be making the change from the 3-4 to the 4-3 and with little talent there, this switch will take time. The linebackers have some individual talent – E.J. Junior, Freddie Joe Nunn, Anthony Bell – but rarely play as a unit. The only bright spot seems to be the secondary, where impressive guys like Leonard Smith, Cedric Mack, Carl Carter, among others, patrol.

The cards are stacked against this team. A last place finish appears to be their destiny in '87.

more interceptions. We've got to have two or three more impact players."

So what do the Cardinals do on draft day? With the six overall pick, they select quarterback Kelly Stouffer, a fine quarterback for sure, but certainly not worthy of such a high selection. Instead of trading down (many teams were itching for the

trade rumors are more than just that.

Quarterback, though, isn't the only position in flux. On this team, pick just about any position. The running back corps is thin after overused Stump Mitchell and the receivers are poor, considering the physical ailments that have stopped former All Pro Roy Green.

The faces of the NFC East. The Eagles defense (above) clamps onto Marcus Allen. Tony Dorsett (facing page, top left) had to share time with Herschel Walker, but he still gained over 700 yards. Neil Lomax (facing page, top right) parallels the fortunes of his Cards – down and out. Jay Schroeder (facing page, bottom left) emerged as a star, while Lawrence Taylor (facing page, bottom right) reaffirmed his.

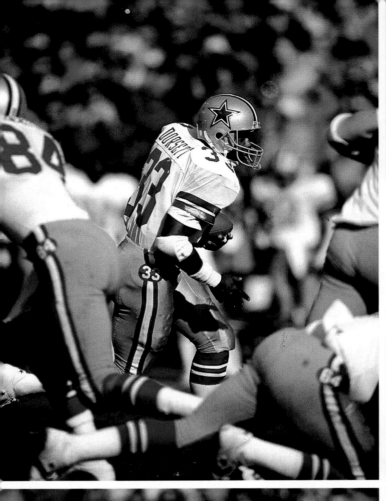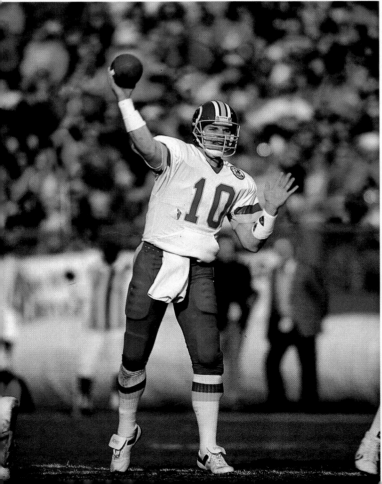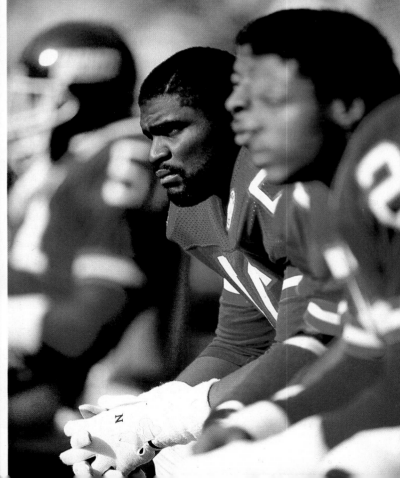

NFC CENTRAL

Chicago Bears

You can be sure that by the time the Bears face the world champion Giants the first game of the season, Chicago coach Mike Ditka will have this bunch growling. The much anticipated showdown between the Bears and Giants in last year's playoffs never came to fruition because of one reason – the Chicago offense.

Even with the departure of Buddy Ryan to the Eagles as head coach, the Bears defensive unit didn't miss a beat with new coordinator Vince Tobin. Tobin, who favors a more controlled defense as opposed to Ryan's 46 pressure "D", nonetheless led his charges to the best defensive record in NFL history. For the regular season, the Bears allowed only 187 points. And with Mike Singletary, Otis Wilson and Wilber Marshall at linebacker and Steve McMichael, Richard Dent and Dan Hampton up front, the Bears will once again be a force against any offense.

Any offense is something the Bears might feel is an improvement after last season's debacle. The problems began when Jim McMahon was bodyslammed to the ground by Green Bay's Charles Martin with a cheapshot. Martin was suspended by the league, but the Chicago offense was never the same without its charismatic leader.

Unfortunately for the Chicago Bears, star quarterback Jim McMahon's (left) dress was better than his health. The flamboyant McMahon missed much of the year with assorted injuries. Walter Payton (facing page, top) continued to add to his NFL rushing lead by gaining 1,333 yards. Willie Gault (facing page, bottom) missed McMahon's throwing ability, but still had his best season in the league and led the Bears receivers with 42 catches.

A trio of quarterbacks – Mike Tomczak, Steve Fuller and Doug Flutie – attempted to fill McMahon's spot with little success. Tomczak, who has the best arm among the three, was inconsistent. Fuller was never a first-string quarterback and Flutie, who was brought in late in the campaign, showed flashes. With a full training camp this season, Flutie expects to wrest the job from the slow-to-recover McMahon.

"I learned the system last year and I know what is expected of me, " says Flutie. "I feel I can come in this year, with the proper training camp, and challenge for the position."

One position that is still unchallenged on Chicago is running back. Walter Payton, the NFL's all-time leading rusher, continues to defy his years in the league, rushing for 1,333 yards in 1986. He has capable backups in second-year man Neal Anderson and third-year pro Thomas Sanders.

But for the Bears to return to the Super Bowl, McMahon will have to play like he did in '85. Or Flutie will have to perform another miracle like he did while at Boston College.

Minnesota Vikings

This could be the season the Vikings once again challenge for supremacy in the NFC Central Division. All the ingredients seem to be in place.

Last season rookie head coach Jerry Burns guided the Vikes to a 9-7 record and only heartbreaking losses separated Minnesota from the playoffs. Of the seven Viking losses a year ago, the average defeat was by

The fight for survival in the NFC Central Division started in the pits. For the Tampa Bay Buccaneers, though, the entire 1986 season was the pits. The Bucs won only two games while losing 14. The only thing they didn't lose was the chance to draft Vinny Testaverde and hopefully turn the franchise around. The Bears, meanwhile, had the exact opposite record, winning 14 and losing two. Their favorite feast? Easy pickins' like the Bucs.

eight points. In three games against playoff powers like the Giants, the Redskins and the Browns, Minnesota lost by a collective 11 points. The job this season will be to turn those close losses into close victories.

The heart of this Viking team is at quarterback, where Tommy Kramer rebounded from a miserable 1985 to earn Pro Bowl honors in '86. The Rice-product finished the season with 3,522 yards passing and 24 touchdowns. His 92.6 quarterback rating was also the best in the NFL.

To make life easy for a thrower like Kramer, the Vikings have put together one of the best receiving corps in football. Start with game-breaker Anthony Carter (686 yards receiving), add Steve Jordan (859), sprinkle in Leo Lewis (600) and there's the makings of a fine mix. Then throw in running back Darrin Nelson (593) and another wide out, Hassan Jones (570) and this is a unit that could turn a defense into an upside down cake.

"As far as the offense is concerned," says Kramer, "this is the most depth we've had at wide receiver and offensive line since I've been here."

The defense isn't too shabby either, with standouts like Keith Millard and Gerald Robinson on the defensive line. Millard led the team in sacks with 10½ and his pressure on opposing quarterbacks helped the Vikes finish second in the NFC in the all-important takeaway/giveaway ratio.

Now all coach Jerry Burns wants to see in 1987 is the steady improvement the Vikes showed throughout 1986. If he gets that, and if Kramer has another solid season, the Vikes may very well push Chicago for the Central Division championship.

The Chicago Bears defense might have been fantastic during their Super Bowl season of '85, but it was even better last year under the tutelage of Vince Tobin. Chicago set a league record by allowing the fewest number of points in a season, 187. Left: Dave Duerson (22) and Wilber Marshall (50) stuff the Bucs.

Detroit Lions

For a team with a lot of talent, the Detroit Lions didn't get much out of it as they finished 1986 with a dismal 5-11 record. The responsibility for making that talent work – head coach Darryl Rogers – is now in the hot seat in Detroit. A poor start or another subpar season by the Lions and Rogers will be thrown to the Tigers.

For Rogers to take control of this team, he'll have to figure out a solution to the muddled situation at quarterback. The Lions made much-heralded Iowa quarterback Chuck

Long their number one selection in the draft last season and Long didn't get much opportunity to show his talents. Instead, Rogers used heady veteran Eric Hipple much of the way, and when Hipple went down with an injury, Rogers inserted the much-travelled Joe Ferguson. With pressure from management to play Chuck Long, expect the big, strapping signalcaller to get the shot at QB.

The player the Lions selected after Long, running back Garry James from LSU, was a pleasant surprise. James, a power runner, rambled for 688 yards in his freshman season. Teamed with standout fullback James Jones, the Lions are assured of a solid tandem in the backfield.

"Most people let their tailback lead the way, but we've gotten it from every

position," says Rogers. "I think J.J. should be a 1,000-yard rusher and a guy who catches at least 50 passes. And I believe Garry can match those numbers."

Paving the way for James and Jones is arguably the best offensive line in football. Not only may they be the best, but they're certainly the biggest. With Lomas Brown (6-4, 282), Harvey Salem (6-6, 285), Steve Mott (6-3, 275), Keith Dorney (6-5, 290) and Rich Strenger (6-7, 288), the Lions are set up front for years.

The defense is another story and its an area Rogers and his staff will have to work on. Their best player on "D" is Keith Ferguson and he recorded only nine sacks a year ago.

But the main problem is at quarterback. Will it be Long or Hipple? The right answer could save Rogers his job.

Green Bay Packers

For what seems like the umpteenth time since the Packer glory days of the late 1960s, Green Bay appears to be a team in transition. A year ago head coach Forrest Gregg and the Packers' management decided the team needed another face lift so out went the veterans and in came the youngsters.

On the way out were veterans Lynn Dickey, Paul Coffman, Greg

Koch and Mike Douglass. In their place was a host of no-name players with less talent but more enthusiasm. Unfortunately, the results were the same, as the Pack finished another dreary campaign with a 4-12 record. And before this season even began, James Lofton, the team's best player, was traded to the Los Angeles Raiders for a draft pick.

Despite the unpopular move of cutting long-time quarterback Lynn Dickey, the Packers seemed to make the right choice because of the sudden development of raw Randy Wright. The relative unknown from Wisconsin stepped in and displayed the arm, accuracy, poise and leadership Gregg was hoping for when he gave Dickey his walking papers.

Wright responded to the promotion by finishing third in the team's history with 263 completions and over 3,000 yards passing.

Even though Wright had a fine season, the Packers offense still dragged behind the rest, finishing 26th in the NFL in scoring. Much of the problem, however, is due to the lack of a bonafide running game. The Pack's offense scored just eight rushing touchdowns and ranked only 18th in the running category. Help is needed in this unit with only second-year man Keith Davis a sure thing. On draft day, though, the Pack took a big step toward improving this unit by selecting the best running back in college, Auburn's Brent Fullwood.

As porous as the offense was a year ago, the defense was even worse. Other than Charles Martin, who was suspended for ending Bears' quarterback Jim McMahon's season with a late body-slam, the line was less than adequate. And with grizzled

Give me the hotline. No it's not the president, but the Vikings linebacker Scott Studwell, talking on the phone with his leaders, the Minnesota coaching staff. Garry James (facing page, top) was a welcome addition to the Detroit backfield as he gained 688 yards in his rookie season. Steve Bartkowski, who retired after last season, feels the wrath of Detroit defensive lineman Curtis Greer (facing page, bottom).

veteran Ezra Johnson, the team's best pass rusher, slowing down noticeably, the Pack needs more depth on the line. As Gregg readily admits, "this is an area where we need more players."

Nobody is expecting Green Bay to challenge for the Central Division title in 1987. Their best hope is that the Pack is simply competitive.

Tampa Bay Bucs

The carousel keeps turning in Tampa and another new era is ready to begin for the Bucs. Exit Leeman Bennett. Enter high-profile Ray Perkins. If the Bucs can't win, the management figures, it might as well try to draw some fans.

To help Perkins bring those fans into the Buccaneers' playground is the NFL's number one draft choice Vinny Testaverde. Last season the Bucs screwed up by letting Bo Jackson, the Heisman Trophy winner of 1985, play professional baseball. This time they didn't let dollars stand in the way of college's best football player.

Randy Wright (facing page) found a home at quarterback for the Green Bay Packers although he has one uninvited guest. The Bears lived on the run in '86 with Jim McMahon's injury and led the NFL in rushing yardage for the third straight season. Above: the Bucs try to stop Walter Payton.

Testaverde, the former University of Miami standout, won the Heisman Trophy in '86 and forced the Bucs to fork over a multi-million dollar contract for his services. The highly-touted passer is expected to bring instant results to Tampa. While he is the best quarterback prospect since 1984, scouts feel Vinny won't bring the instant results Tampa management hopes. But one thing he has already done is force former starting QB Steve Young out of the pocket and onto the sidelines. And not even the Tampa sidelines. As soon as Testaverde inked a contract, the Bucs traded Young to the 49ers for draft picks.

With that done, the Bucs should

start worrying about what to do on the field. Last season the offense ranked 27 overall. The rushing game was more than adequate – the Bucs ranked number 12 in the NFL on the ground – with underrated James Wilder carrying the ball. The passing game, however, was next-to-last in the NFL, and in midseason former coach Leeman Bennett released high-salaried (and also highly talented) wide receiver Kevin House and tight end Jimmie Giles. Testaverde should immediately help the passing game, but who's he going to throw to?

If you thought the offense was bad, just take a look at the defense. Last season the Bucs finished dead last in the NFL in stopping the opposition. They were 28th against the run and 24 against the pass. The only positive is that, after Testaverde, management drafted a slew of defensive players (they somehow managed to get 20 draft picks) and hopefully a few could step in and give immediate help.

Yeah, the Bucs will be bad again. But at least they should be more entertaining this year.

NFC WEST

Los Angeles Rams

When rookie quarterback Jim Everett took over as Rams signalcaller late last season, the offense began slowly to change. Eric Dickerson, the NFL's best running back, wasn't carrying the ball on every down. The Rams were no longer a one-dimensional team. Everett, who was traded to Los Angeles after holding out as the Oilers number one pick, put his powerful arm to work and started to give the Rams a passing game. Watch out, NFL.

"Jim Everett is the future for the Rams," says L.A. head coach John Robinson. "Certainly he has a lot to learn, but from a poise and maturity standpoint, I'm very impressed." He's not the only one. In his first game, Everett came off the bench in week 11 and threw three touchdown passes. His appearance in the lineup will give the Rams the balanced attack they lacked for so many years. And with an equal distribution of passing and running, opposing defensive coordinators will spend their nights

John Robinson (above) exhorted his troops, but the Rams still finished second and lost to the Bears in the playoffs. Eric Dickerson's life was turned upside down at times in '86 (left), but most of the time Dickerson was a stright shooter thanks to the blocking of Irv Pankey (overleaf).

trying to figure out a way to stop the Rams.

None of them, however, has been able to devise a plan to stop Dickerson. For the third time in his four-year career, Dickerson led the NFL in rushing. The former SMU Pony carried the ball 404 times for 1,821 yards, 300 more than his nearest competitor. His rushing total was the sixth highest in NFL history and he set

club records for career rushing yards (6,968) and career touchdowns (57). And when Dickerson needs a breather, the Rams don't lose much when Barry Redden enters the lineup. The former first-round draft choice rushed for 467 yards and caught 28 passes for 217 yards.

The most encouraging news for Everett and Dickerson, though, is the offensive line. Three of the Rams linemen – guard Dennis Harrah, tackle Jackie Slater and center Doug Smith – played in the Pro Bowl. And two others, last season's number one draft pick Tom Newberry and tackle Irv Pankey, may be on the way.

The Rams defense is not shy of talent, either. Los Angeles finished with the fifth best defense in the

Roger Craig (below) suffered through an injury-plagued season, although his intensity level was never on injured reserve. The Rams defense was the team's strength as James Jones (facing page, top) and Eric Hipple (facing page, bottom) find out the hard way.

league and possesses one of the top secondaries in football. Cornerbacks LeRoy Irvin and Jerry Gray both made the Pro Bowl and anchored a defense that intercepted 28 passes.

There is no real weak spot on these Rams. A trip to the conference championship would be no surprise.

The team's backup quarterback, Jeff Kemp, played well in place of Montana, but he also sustained an injury, missing four games. Quarterbacks weren't the only ones affected. As a team, the Niners' starters missed a culmulative 61 games due to injury.

But somehow, head coach Bill Walsh pulled the team together, enough to win the NFC West with a 10-5-1 record. And this season, with all the regulars healthy again, the 49ers should battle with the powerful Rams and the upstart Saints for the divisional crown.

San Francisco 49ers

There wasn't a team in the NFL that overcame more adversity that the San Francisco 49ers. The team's starting quarterback, Joe Montana, who is the highest rated passer in NFL history, was sidelined early in the campaign with a severe back injury. At the time, doctors feared for his football career.

Eric Dickerson rushed for an NFL-leading 1,821 yards (above) and kept his shirt in the process. Joe Montana (facing page) made the most amazing comeback of the season, rebounding from back surgery to finish second in the NFC in passing and completing 62.2 percent of the throws.

Nobody deserved a crown more than Joe Montana did last season. The nine-year veteran suffered ruptured discs and missed eight weeks after back surgery. His speedy recovery baffled doctors and when Montana took the field in the 10th game, his performance even baffled his teammates. All Montana did was connect on 13 of 19 passes for 270 yards and three touchdowns. He

finished the season as the second-rated NFC passer behind Tommy Kramer.

"He demonstrated great determination and sacrifice in returning to the lineup following back surgery," says Walsh. "His offseason work is on schedule and he has gained back most of the weight that he lost through his physical ordeal" (Montana played 15 pounds under his usual weight).

Just to make sure, Walsh traded for former phenom Steve Young, who didn't satisfy Tampa Bay's management with his slow development, leading to the Bucs drafting Vinny Testaverde with the number one draft pick.

To make things easy for Montana, the Niners unleashed Jerry Rice full-force onto the NFL. The former Mississippi Valley State star exploded in his second NFL season, becoming the league's top deep threat. All Rice did was catch 86 passes (to lead the NFC, second in the NFL behind the Raiders' Todd Christensen's 95 receptions) for 1,570 yards and 15 touchdowns.

"He is certainly one of the best players in football, regardless of position," says Walsh. "He is emerging as a team leader and has tremendous strength and stamina."

He wasn't the only one with strength and stamina. The entire defense seemed to have it. San Francisco was ranked as the sixth best defense in the league and third against the run. The front line of rookie Charles Haley (he led the Niners in sacks with 12), All Pro nose tackle Michael Carter and veteran Jeff Stover was an overwhelming unit. But then again, so were the linebackers and the defensive backs.

And the only way the Niners won't be back in the playoffs is if Joe Montana's back doesn't hold up.

New Orleans Saints

Start waving the red flags. The Saints are marching in and, unlike years past, these Saints are marching to a different drummer. The drummer is head coach Jim Mora, who, along with general manager Jim Finks, will bring the Saints their first winning season — ever.

The former USFL coach, who won two titles in his three campaigns in the disbanded league, brings a winning and competitive attitude to Cajun country. As their opponents found out last season, the Saints are no longer an easy win – if they are a win at all. In his first campaign in New Orleans, Mora brought respectability to go along with a 7-9 record. During the season, they beat both the Rams and 49ers, their chief contenders in the NFC West Division, and in the process broke or tied over 30 team records.

Not only were the Saints surprising as a team, but Reuben Mayes, a third round pick last season, blossomed to become the NFL's rookie of the year. Mayes outgained all rookies in rushing as he ran for 1,353 yards, fourth in the NFL. He also scored eight touchdowns and was second in the NFC in yards per carry average with a 4.7.

"He has cutback ability that bleeds yardage from opponents," says Mora. "You don't notice it at first, but then you realize he's almost never stopped for a negative gain. He's surrounded, then he squirts for another two yards."

One of the reasons Mayes was so successful is the play of the Saints unheralded offensive line. They don't get the ink that others do, but Stan Brock, Chuck Commiskey, Steve Korte, Brad Edelman and Bill Contz form a fabulous unit that should continue to dominate defensive lines.

The offensive line isn't the only unit that doesn't get the publicity it should. The Saints defense, which ranked 14th overall, but fourth against the run, is led by an outstanding corps of linebackers. The number one guy is All Pro Rickey Jackson, who led the club with 117 tackles. Joining Jackson are Sam Mills, Alvin Toles and James Haynes. The foursome is young and formidable.

Just like the rest of the team.

Atlanta Falcons

This is a strange organization all right. In 1976, they fire head coach Marion Campbell. In 1986, they fire head coach Dan Henning. His replacement? That's right, Marion Campbell. Oh, well, you know what they say. If at first you don't suceed ...

At least this try Campbell should have the horses to field a respectable team. In fact, if the Falcons can get lucky, they might even sneak into the playoffs. Last year the Falcons began grooming young David Archer as their first-string quarterback. The kid from Soda Springs, Idaho, had troubles at times, but overall he did a fine job. For the season, he hit on 51.0 percent of his passes for 2,007 yards and 10 touchdowns. The only problem is that Atlanta drafted highly-touted quarterback Chris Miller with its number one pick. Archer should begin the season number one but, if he gets off to a slow start, a quarterback controversy might develop.

There is no question who is the Falcons number one running back. Not only is Gerald Riggs the Falcons' best, but he is among the NFL's best. Riggs earned a spot in his second straight Pro Bowl by garnering 1,327 yards and leading Atlanta to the third-best rushing attack in the league.

Paving the way for Riggs is one of the NFL's top offensive lines. The kingpin of the line is Pro Bowler Bill Fralic. The 6-5, 280 pound University of Pittsburgh graduate is a runaway freight train on sweeps and he steamrolls anything in his path. Mike Kenn is the other Pro Bowl lineman and he has started 130 consecutive games.

The defensive line may be just as good as its offensive counterparts. The unit helped the Falcons become the seventh-ranked defense in the league and it is led by a trio of former first round draft picks. Rick Bryan and Mike Gann are the defensive ends, while Tony Casillas, last season's second overall pick, is the nose tackle. These guys are the heart of the defense and an outstanding performance is needed by all three because the linebackers and secondary is not up to par.

Nevertheless, this should be an interesting season in Atlanta. And mostly for positive reasons.

The San Francisco defense was sixth overall in the league, something Billy "White Shoes" Johnson (facing page, top) knows first-hand. David Archer (facing page, bottom) worked his way into the starting quarterback position for the Falcons and found the road a bit bumpy at times.

AFC EAST

Tony Eason of the New England Patriots developed into one of the best young quarterbacks in the National Football League. Eason's arm (facing page) accounted for 19 touchdowns as the former number one draft pick finished third in the AFC in passing by throwing for 3,328 yards. Eason also smoothly directed the Patriots offense (above), although he didn't get much help from a ground game that finished dead last in the league.

Indianapolis Colts

Something strange happened on the Colts path to Vinny Testaverde – they won. With an 0-13 record after the first 13 weeks of the season, the Colts felt assured they would get the draft rights to University of Miami's Heisman Trophy-winning quarterback. But after the 13th straight loss, the Colts management dismissed head coach Rod Dowhower and brought in disciplinarian Ray Meyer. The result was three wins in the final three weeks. The only loss was Testaverde, who was scooped up by the 2-14 Tampa Bay Buccaneers.

Instead of the number one pick, the Colts settled for being the bridesmaid and they choose Alabama's all-American linebacker Cornelius Bennett. Described favorably as a Lawrence Taylor-type player, Bennett may have to perform at that level for the Indianapolis fans to forget Testaverde.

The reason Vinny is not preparing for a season in Indianapolis is another quarterback, Gary Hogeboom. Injured most of the season with a shoulder separation, Hogeboom came back strong in those final three games to lead the Colts to victory. Against Buffalo, the former Cowboy hit 23 of

33 passes for 318 yards and two touchdowns, and in the final game versus the Raiders, he was 19-30 for 240 yards and two more TDs. He will shoulder the burden of the Colts offense this season.

Indianapolis' running game was dealt a blow in the offseason as, a day before the draft, the team's leading runner, Randy McMillan (609 yards rushing with 34 receptions), was in an automobile accident that puts his future in doubt.

Hogeboom will have no such trouble with his receivers, who have developed into a splendid corps. Bill Brooks, the AFC Rookie of the Year, was a steal as a fourth round draft pick in '86, catching 65 passes for 1,131 yards and eight TDs. His partner, Matt Bouza, was the team's offensive MVP by hauling in 71 passes for 830 yards

The success of the defense, though, will likely decide whether the Colts become contenders or remain pretenders. The team ranked 25th overall in 1986 and 26th against the pass. The addition of Bennett can do nothing but help. The only other legitimate blue-chippers on the defense are linebackers Duane Bickett, who was the team's MVP, and Barry Krauss, who missed most of last season with major knee surgery.

In retrospect, maybe it was the best thing for the franchise winning those final three games. After all, the offense may be average, but the defense is simply bad.

New England Patriots

Considering the problems the Patriots had in 1986, it's amazing that they won the East Division with an 11-5 record and nearly beat Super Bowl participant Denver in the playoffs.

The Pats, who played in the Super Bowl in '85 against the Bears, suffered an enormous number of injuries and a complete breakdown in the ground game. New England rode the running of Craig James and Tony Collins to attain the NFL's top rushing game in '85, and it was that performance that helped young quarterback Tony Eason develop by alleviating the pressure on the passing game. But last season, the Pats went from one to done in a hurry; New England finished dead last in rushing in the league.

Part of that problem was the retirement of All Pro guard John Hannah. Another part was the injury to superb blocking tight end Lin Dawson, who was injured in the Super Bowl. But James, who rushed for only 427 yards and Collins, who garnered 412, ran for over 100 yards combined twice, an abysmal total. However, help is on the way.

New England concentrated its draft on picking up its rushing game, selecting an offensive lineman (Bruce Armstrong) and a strong fullback (Bob Perryman). Both should help the Pats immediately.

The Pats needed no help with their passing game (they finished with the fourth rated passing game in the NFL) as Eason continued to develop into one of the game's outstanding signalcallers. The former Illinois first round pick closed 1986 as the third-rated passer in the conference with a completion percentage of 61.6. His problem in prior seasons has been the interception, but Eason threw only 10 while tossing 19 touchdowns and passing for 3,328 yards.

Eason didn't do it alone, as his wide receivers, Stanley Morgan and Irving Fryar, are among the best in the league. Morgan, who was named All Pro, caught 84 balls for 1,491 yards and 10 touchdowns. Fryar wasn't as productive, but he did haul in 43 tosses, including a 69-yard TD.

As usual, the Pats defense was among the best, although they did have some trouble defensing the run. New England placed 24th versus the rush but only five teams in the league played the pass better. Injuries to key defenders like Andre Tippett, Steve Nelson, and Kenneth Sims really hurt this unit. If the defense is healthy in 1987, New England should have no trouble stopping the opposition.

And if the rushing game improves as it should, the Pats will certainly take the East and be a force in the playoffs.

The Jets' biggest problem was their defense. Injuries struck down perennial All Pros Joe Klecko, Lance Mehl and Mark Gastineau and opposing teams (right) found that they could fly over the Jets easily, as Roger Craig of the 49ers does here.

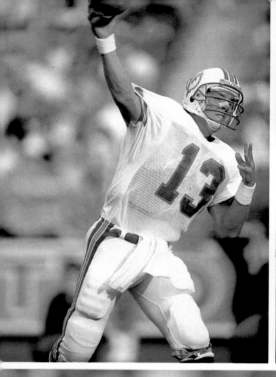

Miami Dolphins

You know Miami can score. After all, they do have Dan Marino. But question for 1987 is, can the Dolphins stop anybody. The answer will decide if Miami are good enough to make the playoffs.

Last season the Dolphins couldn't defense a pee-wee team. Miami had the 26th rated defense in the NFL and they were consistent. The pass defense was ranked 22nd and the rush defense was rated 27th. Whether it was by air or ground, these Dolphins just drowned.

But Miami, which opens its new stadium in the exhibition season, spent the offseason trying to shore up its defense. Before the draft, head coach Don Shula tabbed a new defensive coordinator, Tom Olivadotti. Then, in the draft, Shula picked defensive lineman John Bosa of Boston College, who scouts feel can step in and produce immediately.

If Bosa turns out as good as last season's rookie gem, linebacker John Offerdahl, the Dolphins will be thrilled. Drafted in the second round from Western Michigan, Offerdahl stepped right into the starting lineup – and not

surprises and that was the good news. Dan Marino is still the NFL's most dangerous quarterback, and he has the most dangerous pair of wide receivers in Mark Clayton and Mark Duper. Marino led the AFC in passing, completing 60.7 percent of his throws for 4,746 yards and an amazing 44 touchdowns. In comparison, only one other quarterback in the league – Washington's Jay Schroeder – passed for over 4,000 yards and nobody threw for even 30 touchdowns.

And the Marks Brothers were the beneficiaries of Marino's talents.

The faces of the AFC East. Miami's Dan Marino (facing page, top left) showed once again why he is the best, while Buffalo's Jim Kelly (facing page, top center) and New York's Ken O'Brien (facing page, bottom) follow in his steps. Mark Duper (facing page, top right) caught 67 of Marino's passes even though the Dolphs couldn't ice a playoff spot (above).

only for the Dolphins. Offerdahl's performance was so compelling that the NFL named him as starter in the Pro Bowl game. His credentials? One hundred thirty-five tackles (109 solo), two sacks, three fumbles forced, eight passes defensed and an interception.

The offense didn't have any

Duper caught 67 passes for 1,313 yards and 11 touchdowns. He also averaged a lofty 19.6 yards per catch. On the opposite side of the line, Clayton hauled in 60 passes for 1,150 yards and 10 touchdowns. He, too, riddled defenses for over 19 yards per reception.

There is no question that Miami can put the points on the board. The question is can they stop the opposition. The answer will determine whether the Dolphins will play in the postseason or remain home for the holidays.

New York Jets

Which team is the real New York Jets? Is it the bunch that went 11-1 in the first 12 weeks of the season and crushed the opposition with ease? Or is it the 0-5 sad sacks who couldn't get

The 1986 version of the Miami Dolphins (facing page) were a long drink of water from first place in the AFC East and had to sweat just to reach the .500 mark for the campaign. New England (below) was buoyed by a strong defense even though starters like Steve Nelson and Andre Tippett missed action due to injuries.

out of their own way? Unfortunately for the Jets fans, New York appears closer to the latter.

The reason? Injuries. New York suffered major injuries in '86 that will likely wreak havoc in '87. Joe Klecko, the best nose tackle in the NFL, suffered a severe knee injury that required reconstructive knee surgery. Lance Mehl, a Pro Bowl linebacker, suffered a knee injury that required reconstructive knee surgery. Same injury, different All Pro. Neither will be available until midseason of this year at best.

But that's not all. Marty Lyons, a big contributor to the Jets line, had surgery on both of his shoulders in the offseason. His return is a question mark. Mark Gastineau, the perennial All Pro and sack leader, was reduced to a mere shell of himself last season by a nagging abdominal pull and he recorded only two sacks. He also underwent knee surgery in the offseason. The good news is that Gastineau should be at full speed by training camp.

All the injuries added up to the 26th-rated defense in the league, 28th against the pass. The Jets did take measures to improve that by selecting Alex Gordon, a big linebacker out of Cincinnati in the second round of the draft, and blitzing linebacker Onzy Elam was the third choice. The two should have an immediate impact on the Jets.

So should the Jets number one draftee. Roger Vick, a bruising back from Texas A&M, will finally give the Jets a solid complement to Freeman McNeil in the backfield. The 230-pound fullback can rush, block and catch the ball.

If quarterback Ken O'Brien can overcome the slump that ruined the end of the season for him, Vick should be receiving many footballs. O'Brien started strongly for the Jets, giving them the top rated passing game for much of the season. He faltered badly down the stretch, although his overall numbers are still impressive. O'Brien completed 62.2 percent of his passes for 3,690 yards

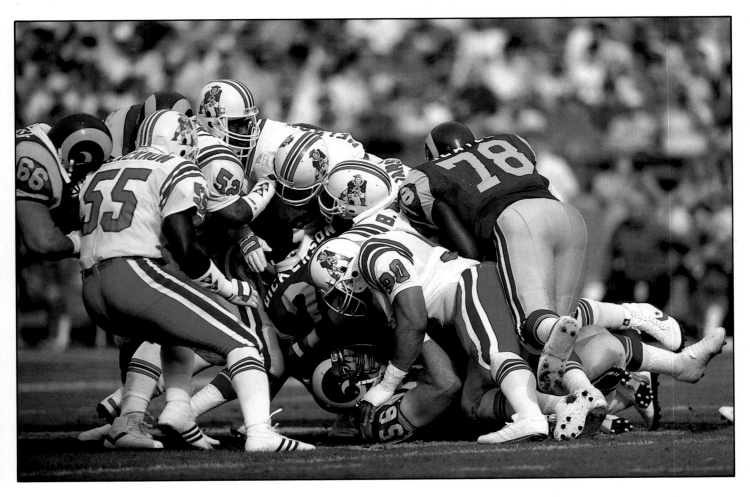

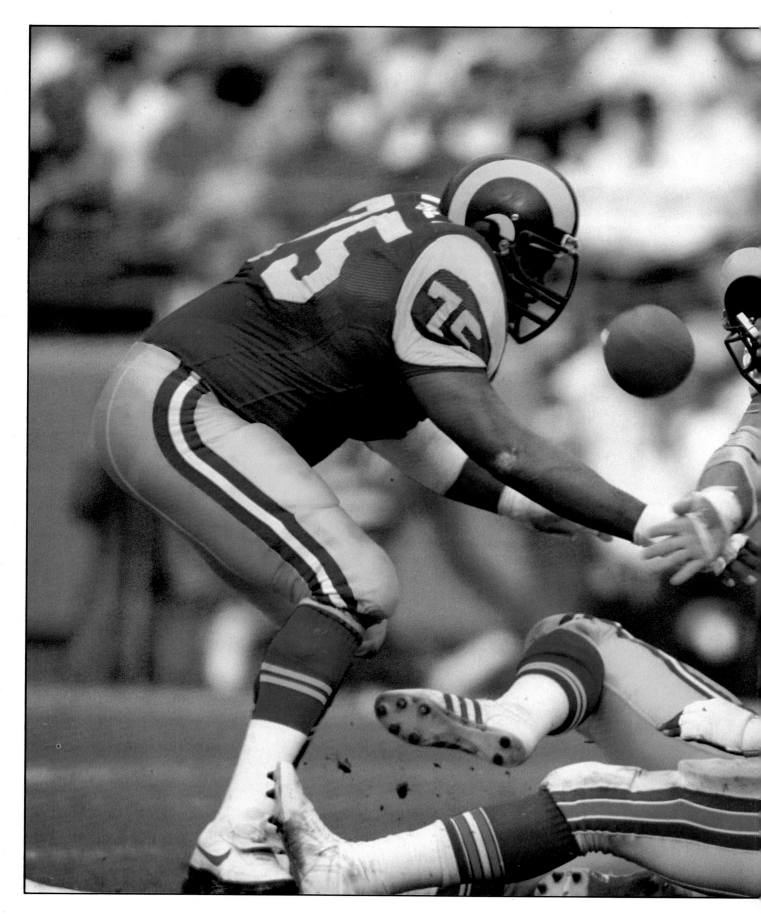

and 25 touchdowns. Twenty of those TDs went to his wide receiver combination of Al Toon and Wesley Walker. Toon, the number one draft choice in '85, caught 85 passes for 1,176 yards and eight touchdowns. Walker, who benefited from having Toon opposite him, hauled in 49 balls for 1,016 yards and 12 touchdowns. Even tight end Mickey Shuler chipped in, receiving 69 passes for 675 yards and four TDs.

With another year of experience, O'Brien and the offense should be all right. The main project for head coach Joe Walton, though, is making some sense out of the muddled defensive situation. A situation that seems unlikely to come together fast enough for the Jets to make the playoffs again.

Buffalo Bills

Watch out. This is a team that could surprise a lot of people in 1987. Sure the Bills had a typical Buffalo season, finishing the campaign with a dismal 4-12 record. Sure the team placed 19th overall on defense and 24th overall on offense. Sure, this is a team that finished with a 1-7 divisional record. Equally sure, the Bills could be the most improved team from last season.

Leading the Bills will be former USFL great Jim Kelly, who took over in Buffalo without the benefit of training camp. The much-heralded quarterback stepped in immediately, took his lumps, but also brought some sense of direction to the team. Buffalo now knows that Kelly, who has never been shy about his abilities, is the leader of the team and they're counting on him to lead them to the playoffs.

If last season — his first in the NFL — is any indication of his abilities to run the Buffalo offense, the Bills are in good shape. As an NFL rookie, the former University of Miami product

A scene not played very often by the Dolphins last season: Los Angeles Rams star running back Eric Dickerson has the ball jarred loose by a Dolphin defender while offensive lineman Irv Pankey dives for the pigskin.

73

completed 59.4 percent of his passes for 3,593 yards and 22 touchdowns. The statistics are impressive considering that Kelly had to play it conservative, the way former head coach Hank Bullough wanted it. But that problem won't be around, because Bullough was fired in midseason and replaced by Marv Levy.

Kelly even has some talent to work with when Levy wants to open up the offense. Running back Greg Bell ran the ball only 90 times, but gained 377 yards for a 4.2 average. Bell is also an excellent receiver, as is his backfield partner Rob Riddick. Riddick emerged as the Bills' top back, rushing the ball for 632 yards and catching 49 passes for 468 yards. Both were team highs.

A lot of the improvement, though, will come on the defense. Most observers feel that Buffalo had the top draft in the NFL, landing at least two possible impact players. The first, linebacker Shane Conlan from Penn State, is the man Buffalo coveted and he should make an immediate impact. The second, defensive back Nate Odomes, is an outstanding athlete and he should help the 27th-ranked pass defense.

For the first time in years, the Bills are a legitimate threat on the football field. Just watch and see.

The Jets best rushing threat, Freeman NcNeil (above), had a rocky start to his season. The injury-prone running back from UCLA suffered a separated shoulder against the New England Patriots and missed several games. Here, McNeil is gathered up by San Francisco 49ers defensive lineman Manu Tuiasosopo. New York expected big things from JoJo Townsell (facing page) after the diminutive receiver signed following the demise of the USFL. Townsell, though, didn't participate much in the offense and when he did, the ball slipped through his fingers often.

74

AFC CENTRAL

Cleveland Browns

So close yet so far. That was the feeling in Cleveland last January when the Denver Broncos, led by John Elway, drove 98 yards in the final five minutes of the fourth quarter to tie the AFC Championship Game before winning it in overtime. Thus, the Browns were one drive away from the Super Bowl. And this season? Nothing short of that trip to the Super Bowl will be acceptable.

This season will be a better test to see exactly how good these Browns are. Last year, despite compiling the AFC's best record, 12-4, they faced the NFL's easiest schedule. The Browns' opponents had a combined record of 111-145. But don't expect the Browns to fold this year; they just have too much talent.

And that superior talent begins at quarterback with Bernie Kosar. In only his second season in the league, the 23-year-old University of Miami graduate completed 58.4 percent of his passes for 3,854 yards. He had two monster games – 32-50 for 401 yards versus Miami and 28-46 for 414 yards against Pittsburgh – in the regular season before a virtuoso performance in the last 10 minutes of the Jets playoff game, when Bernie singlehandedly brought the Browns back from certain defeat. He was also equally impressive against Denver in the championship game.

"Kosar was impressive when we played him in that championship game," says Denver coach Dan Reeves. "I didn't realize he could throw the ball with that velocity. You had to be impressed with what he'd done, but until I saw him warming up before the game, I didn't realize that he had that strong of an arm."

The Browns, though, were not a one-man show. The defense, especially the linebackers and secondary, were outstanding. So good were the middle men that the Browns traded All Pro Chip Banks to San Diego for the Chargers, first round draft choice. With that selection, the Browns picked another linebacker – Mike Junk of Duke – whose ferocious demeanor reminds people of former Steeler great Jack Lambert. Joining Junkin will be Clay Matthews, Eddie Johnson and Anthony Griggs. Not a soft spot anywhere.

Just like the secondary. Despite the offseason death of safety Don Rogers due to cocaine abuse, the Browns still had one of the finest defensive backfields in the game. The corners – Hanford Dixon and Frank Minnifield – were the best combination in the league and the safeties – Ray Ellis and Chris Rockins – were stalwarts also.

The Browns will have a tougher path to the Conference Championship game this season, but the talent is there to achieve it.

Houston Oilers

The Oilers were a very nondescript team following the 1986 campaign, but a long offseason has changed all that. With a draft that brought a wealth of offensive talent, this should be the year Warren Moon blasts off or is permanently grounded.

To help the highly touted former Canadian Football League star, the Oilers drafted banging running back

The Cincinnati Bengals proved to have the best offense in the NFL last season and its leader was quarterback Boomer Esiason (right). The lefthanded hurler from Maryland stymied defenses with his mobility from the pocket and his pinpoint passes as he threw for over 3,900 yards.

Alonzo Highsmith from the University of Miami with its first selection in the draft. With its next pick, Houston plucked speedy receiver Haywood Jeffries from North Carolina State. Added to last season's draft steal, wide receiver Ernest Givens, Moon will have plenty of artillery to blow holes through the opposition.

"I think we have the talent now to start opening it up and throwing the football," says Moon, who has not had the offensive talent in his first two seasons in Houston to do that. "Our defense is starting to play better to where we can gamble a little bit more offensively."

Another reason Moon may be able to gamble more is that he is protected by one of the finest offensive lines in the NFL. Mike Munchak, Jim Romano, Bruce Matthews, Dean Steinkuhler and Kent Hill are all big and talented, with all but Romano Pro Bowl material.

The other side of the line is not as promising, though. Last season the Oilers ranked 13th overall on defense, but a poor 20th against the rush. The blame goes to the spotty line play of starters Ray Childress, Richard Byrd and Doug Smith.

This will be an interesting season in Houston. They've got the offensive talent to win some ballgames and the defense is on the improve. Whether they put it together, though, is another question.

Cincinnati Bengals

By the end of the 1986 season, the Bengals were arguably the hottest team in the league. Their offense, led by quarterback Boomer Esiason, was scorching opponents on its way to leading the league in points scored. The only problem was that the defense forgot it had a job to do. So instead of rolling into the playoffs with

The strength of the Denver Broncos was certainly not on the ground as the Mile High gang finished 20th in the NFL in rushing the football. At right, Gene Lang is handled by the Cleveland Browns defense in the AFC Championship game.

adequate. The linebackers and secondary were equally ineffective and an overall upheaval might be needed.

What won't be needed is another quarterback. Boomer Esiason confidently orchestrated one of the NFL's best big-play offenses, throwing for 24 touchdowns and 3,959 yards. Esiason hit on 58.2 percent of his passes and even has a lower interception rate than Miami's All Pro Dan Marino. "He can really put points on the board" admits Broncos' coach Dan Reeves. "They've got a good scheme and he does it with an awful lot of poise."

And help. The Bengals possess one of the league's best backfield combinations. Led by James Brooks, Cincinnati finished second overall in rushing a year ago. Brooks tip-toed around opponents for 1,087 yards and averaged 5.3 yards per carry. But perhaps his best attribute is his ability to catch passes out of the backfield. Brooks added 686 yards to his rushing total by hauling in 54 receptions. His backfield partners — three bulldozers — were Larry Kinnebrew, Stanley Wilson and Bill Johnson, and they provided the short yardage while blocking a ton for Brooks.

There was never any doubt about Cincy's offensive prowess. If they can find some defense, they can win the Central Division crown.

Pittsburgh Steelers

At the halfway point of the 1986 season, the Steelers looked like one of the worst teams in football. Their record at the time was an un-Steeler-like 2-6 and Chuck Noll's crew looked lost. But the second half proved a charm as Pittsburgh ended the season as one of the hottest in the league. The overall record, 6-10, was not impressive, but nobody that played them in the second half would consider the Steelers a light touch.

A light touch is exactly what Steeler quarterback Mark Malone could use. The athletic signalcaller with the powerful arm fought through some nagging injuries (ligament damage in his thumb) and a horrible first half to rebound and become one of the Steelers' bright spots. In his first four games, Malone completed only

Boomer Esiason (facing page) was able to outrun defenses and throw for 24 touchdown passes at the same time. The Bengals' James Brooks (above) emerged as a legitimate star in '86 as he finished second in the conference in rushing, with 1,087 yards. But his best attribute may have been his receiving, as he hauled in 54 passes for nearly 700 yards.

a high-power offense that could even score on the Giants, the Bengals — with a 10-6 record — watched the playoffs from home.

The Cincinnati defense finished a dismal 20th overall in the league, not a ranking that will likely put them into the playoffs in '87 either. The major problem was the rushing defense, which placed 22nd in the league. Ends Eddie Edwards and Ross Browner have seen better days and nose tackle Tim Krumrie was simply

Denver quarterback John Elway (facing page) has a special way of avoiding pass rushers, even those dressed like Darth Vader. Broncos' placekicker Rich Karlis is one of the few NFL kickers who boot the ball barefoot, and he does it well. In '86, Karlis finished third in the AFC in scoring, with 104 points.

Chargers are still blessed with speedster Wes Chandler and tight end Kellen Winslow, who came back admirably last season following reconstructive knee surgery.

The big change in San Diego last season was on defense. They actually played some. The Chargers' new agressive approach to the defense

helped them lead the NFL in recovering fumbles by snatching 22. And after Saunders took over, the defense stuffed opposing teams to under 100 rushing per game. The unfortunate part is that the player leading the defensive charge last year – rookie sensation Lesley O'Neal – suffered a career-threatening knee

Last season was the year of the Broncos. Rulon Jones (facing page, top) proved to be one of the best defensive linemen in the game, sacking the quarterback 13.5 times. The underrated Denver front line (facing page, bottom) clears the way for Sammy Winder to squirt through a hole. The head man of the Broncos, Dan Reeves (below), led his charges to the Super Bowl. The leader of Denver's Orange Crush defense is all-everything Karl Mecklenburg (#77 overleaf).

injury and should be out all of '87.

Other players, like future star linebacker Billy Ray Smith and lineman Lee Williams have to pick up the slack. And in a draft-day deal, San Diego traded for one of the outstanding linebackers in footballs, Chip Banks.

"We ended our season with great confidence and enthusiasm and that was something that was missing — the enthusiasm, the confidence to know that we can go out there and win ballgames and win the close ones," says Wes Chandler. "So many times

we've played well for three and a half quarters or had a great first half and then gone out and given ball games away. But the last six games of '86 were promising for us."

The only thing San Diego is not promising is an air show.

Kansas City Chiefs

The Kansas City Chiefs made the playoffs last season for the first time since 1971 and, in looking back, it's a wonder how they did it. After all, the

Chiefs had a very unstable situation at quarterback, where third-year disappointment Todd Blackledge and veteran Bill Kenny flip-flopped as the season went along. With the quarterback situation muddled and the fact that Kansas City had one of the poorest rushing game in the NFL, the offense never got untracked and the Chiefs had trouble scoring points.

The only thing that rescued the Chiefs and helped secure the post-season participation was a de-fense and special teams that ranked with the best in football. So good was the special teams play that the units coordinator, Frank Gansz, was given the head coaching job after former mentor John Mackovic was fired following the season.

Nearly one quarter – 10 – of the Chiefs' 43 touchdowns were a direct result of defensive and special teams play. That total was the highest in the

NFL since 1961. The big-play capacity of the defense was so absurd that Lloyd Burress, the team's strong safety, scored four times – three from interception returns and once with a blocked field goal – or once more than the team's heading running back could manage.

With those numbers, it's not surprising that the Chiefs tied for the NFL lead in the takeaway-giveaway stats with 49. And in their wild card playoff game against the Jets, the only score the Chiefs could put on the board was via a blocked punt.

The big offensive problem is at quarterback, with neither Blackledge nor Kenney able to win the job outright. Both signalcallers started eight games last season and each recorded a 5-3 record. However, their total quarterback rating put them only ahead of lowly Pittsburgh in the AFC.

There is no such problem on

defense, where nose tackle Bill Maas registered seven sacks en route to a Pro Bowl invitation. More Pro Bowl invites were handed out in the secondary, with safeties Deron Cherry and Lloyd Burress sharing a plane to Honolulu.

The problem for the Chiefs is not in the defense. But if Kansas City wants to repeat its invitation to the second season, they'll have to find some offense.

The Chiefs and Chargers (above), the doormats of the AFC West the past couple of seasons, began to show signs of progress. The Chiefs even qualified for the playoffs for the first time since 1971. Gary Anderson, a USFL refugee, arrived in San Diego and gave the Chargers' fans hope for the future.

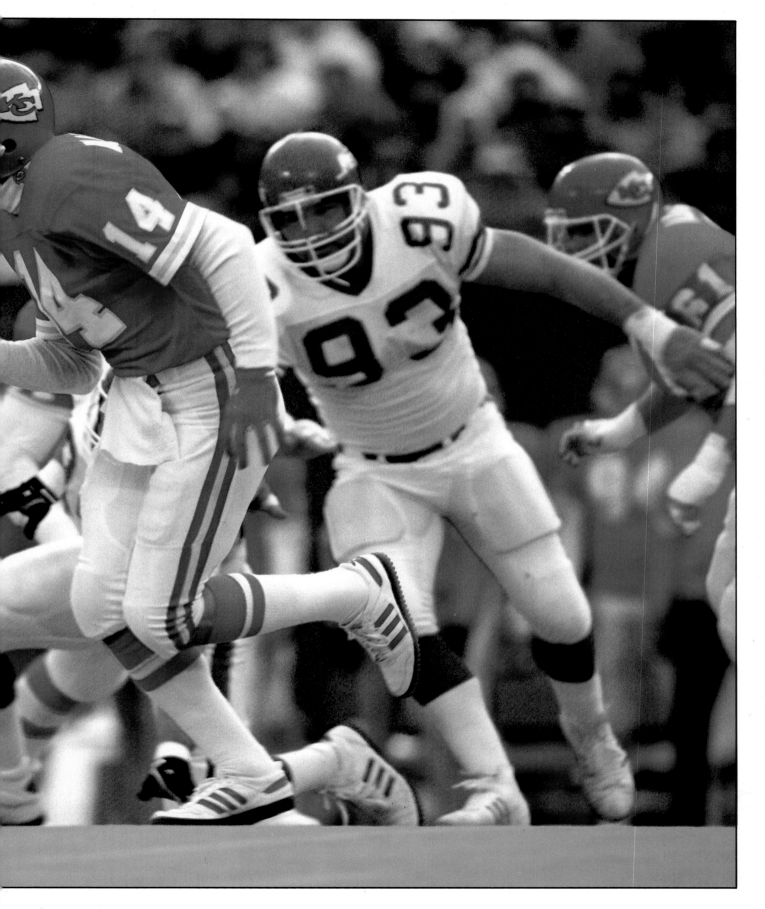

THE LEADERS

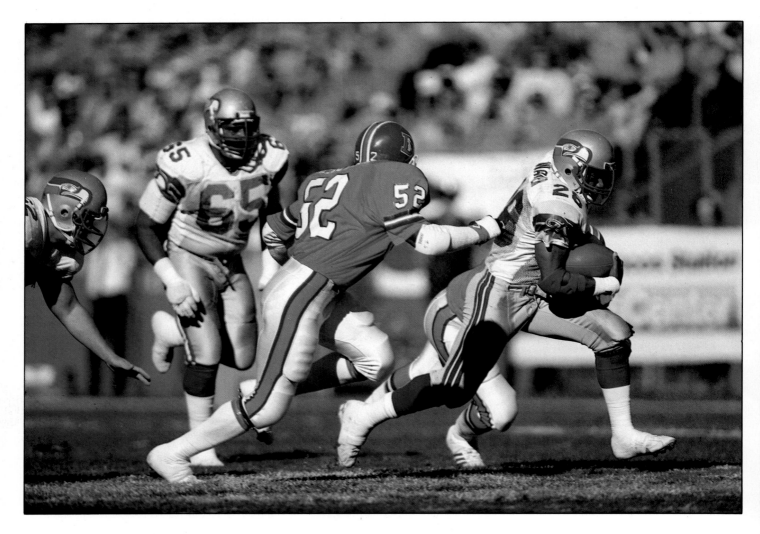

In looking back over the 1986 football season, there weren't many surprises as far as the standings were concerned. The Chicago Bears were once again near the top of the league, winning the NFC Central easily over the second place Vikings with a 14-2 record. In the NFC West, the Rams and 49ers battled it out until the final week before the Niners edged L.A. If there was a surprise in the NFC it was the New York Giants. The surprise wasn't that they captured the East, the surprise was how easily they

handled the competition. The Giants won their first division title since 1963, finishing the regular season 14-2 before destroying the 49ers, Redskins and ultimately, in the Super Bowl, the Denver Broncos.

The American Football Conference showed few surprises, one of them the dismal season of the Miami Dolphins. The Dolphins missed the playoffs for the first time in 6 years, finishing the season with an 8-8 record. The New England Patriots, a year removed from the Super Bowl,

A tale of two backs. Curt Warner (above) and Eric Dickerson (facing page) led their respective conferences in rushing in '87. Warner topped the NFC by over 400 yards and scored 13 touchdowns, while Dickerson grounded out 1,821 yards and 11 touchdowns for the Los Angeles Rams. John Elway of the Broncos (overleaf) not only threw over opposing defenses, but he flew over them as well.

continued to perform admirably, winning the East with an 11-5 mark. In the Central Division, the Cleveland Browns enjoyed a fine campaign, topping the conference with a 12-4 record. And out West, the Broncos, led by John Elway, topped the division with an 11-5 record followed by the surprising 10-6 Chiefs.

Here are the final standings:

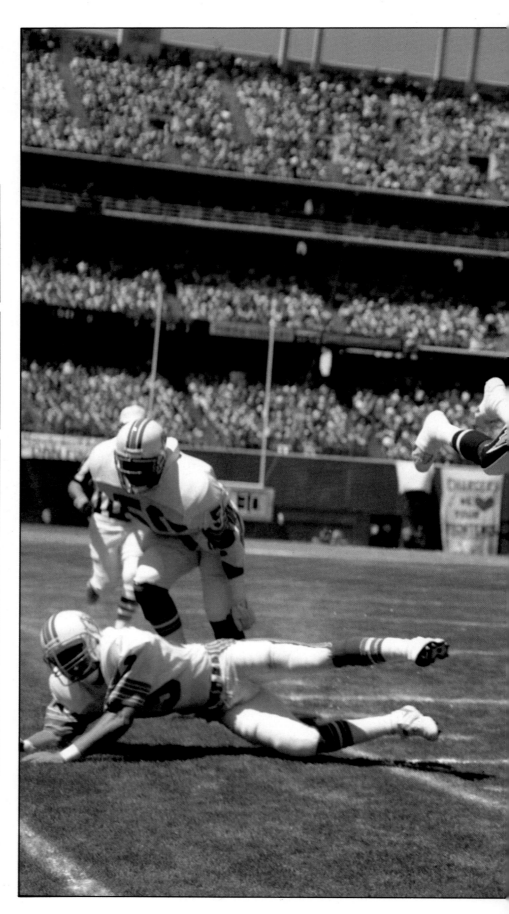

NFC EAST

New York Giants	14-2
Washington Redskins	12-4
Dallas Cowboys	7-9
Philadelphia Eagles	5-10
St. Louis Cardinals	4-11-1

NFC CENTRAL

Chicago Bears	14-2
Minnesota Vikings	9-7
Detroit Lions	5-11
Green Bay Packers	4-12
Tampa Bay Buccaneers	2-14

NFC WEST

San Francisco 49ers	10-5-1
Los Angeles Rams	10-6
Atlanta Falcons	7-8-1
New Orleans Saints	7-9

AFC EAST

New England Patriots	11-5
New York Jets	10-6
Miami Dolphins	8-8
Buffalo Bills	4-12
Indianapolis Colts	3-13

AFC CENTRAL

Cleveland Browns	12-4
Cincinnati Bengals	10-6
Pittsburgh Steelers	6-10
Houston Oilers	5-11

AFC WEST

Denver Broncos	11-5
Kansas City Chiefs	10-6
Seattle Seahawks	10-6
Los Angeles Raiders	8-8
San Diego Chargers	4-12

When the talk turns to rushing, the talk immediately turns to the NFC. Six players from that conference surpassed the 1,000-yard barrier in 1986, compared to only two players in the AFC. Once again, the league's rushing leader was the Rams Eric Dickerson. The former SMU Pony carried the ball for 1,821 yards, over 300 more than the number two guy, Joe Morris of the Giants. Finishing third in rushing was the New Orleans Saints' outstanding rookie, Rueben Mayes. Mayes amassed 1,353 yards on the ground and scored eight touchdowns. The other 1,000-yarders in the NFC were the incomparable Walter Payton, the Falcons' workhorse Gerald Riggs and Washington's George Rogers.

In the AFC, the big story was the amazing comeback of Seattle's Curt Warner. Warner, a year removed from major knee surgery, returned to the form that made him rookie of the year two seasons prior by leading the AFC with 1,481 yards. Warner also led all backs in touchdowns with 13. The only other 1,000-yard man in the AFC was Cincinnati's all-purpose back James Brooks, who finished the season with 1,087 yards on the ground.

Here are the rushing leaders:

Gary Anderson has a style like no other running back in the league. The former USFL star soared (previous pages) over NFL defenses for 442 yards rushing while catching 80 passes for 871 yards. Eric Hipple (facing page) had a surprisingly strong season for the Lions as he finished third in the NFC in passing by completing 63 percent of his tosses. Joe Montana (below) came back from a serious back injury not only to propel the 49ers to a division title, but he also placed second in the NFC in passing.

NFC	
Eric Dickerson	1,821
Joe Morris	1,516
Rueben Mayes	1,353
Walter Payton	1,333
Gerald Riggs	1,327
George Rogers	1,203
James Jones	903
Roger Craig	830
Stump Mitchell	800
Darrin Nelson	793

AFC	
Curt Warner	1,481
James Brooks	1,087
Ernest Jackson	910
Walter Abercrombie	877
Freeman McNeil	856
Lorenzo Hampton	830
Sammy Winder	789
Marcus Allen	759
Kevin Mack	665
Mike Rozier	662

Dan Marino proved once again that he is the NFL's number one quarterback. Despite a sluggish start caused by a training camp holdout, Marino shredded defenses for 44 touchdown passes, the second most by a quarterback after Marino's 48 tosses in 1984. He threw for nearly 5,000 yards, completed over 60 percent of his passes and tossed only 23 interceptions, a reasonable total considering he passed over 600 times. Finishing behind Marino in the AFC was the inconsistent Dave Krieg. Despite being benched in midseason for poor play, Krieg came on at the end and amassed an impressive touchdown to interception ratio (21-11).

In the NFC, Minnesota's Tommy Kramer put on an aerial display as he led the conference in passing. Kramer hit on only 55 percent of his passes, yet averaged over eight yards per completion, the only quarterback other than Boomer Esiason to do that. Kramer also hit for 24 TD passes and threw only 10 interceptions before a late-season injury ended his campaign.

Someone whose campaign was supposed to end was Joe Montana. After suffering a severe back injury early, Montana shocked everyone and returned to action late in the season. And when Montana did, he picked up where he left off, finishing second to Kramer in passing efficiency.

Here are the leaders:

Roger Craig (above) of the San Francisco 49ers is off to the races as he outruns the Jets' Barry Bennett en route to a long gain. Walter Payton of the Bears keeps defying Father Time as the 32-year-old running back rushed for 1,333 yards and eight touchdowns.

AFC	Att.	Comp.	Pct.	Yds.	Tds.	Int.
Dan Marino	623	378	60.7	4,746	44	23
Dave Krieg	375	225	60.0	2,921	21	10
Tony Eason	448	276	61.6	3,328	19	10
Boomer Esiason	469	273	58.2	3,959	24	17
Ken O'Brien	482	300	62.2	3,690	25	20

NFC	Att.	Comp.	Pct.	Yds.	Tds.	Int.
Tommy Kramer	372	208	55.9	3,000	24	10
Joe Montana	307	191	62.2	2,236	8	9
Eric Hipple	305	192	63.0	1,919	9	11
Phil Simms	468	259	55.3	3,487	21	22
Neil Lomax	421	240	57.0	2,583	13	12

Minnesota Vikings quarterback Tommy Kramer (right) had plenty of reasons to smile in '86. The veteran from Rice had his best season in the NFL as he led the league in passing, hitting 55.9 percent of his throws for 3,000 yards and 24 touchdowns. The Raider Todd Christensen (facing page, top) is in a class by himself as far as catching the football is concerned. Last season Christensen led the NFL with 95 receptions for 1,153 yards and eight touchdowns. To think he even did that with the trio of Jim Plunkett, Marc Wilson and Rusty Hilger throwing the ball. Dan Marino (facing page, bottom) continued to show why he is considered the best quarterback in football. The Miami Dolphins star threw for 4,746 yards and 44 touchdowns, the second highest number of TD passes in NFL history. The highest? Marino's mark of 48 in 1984. The Raiders' Marcus Allen has a special way to defeat his opponents. If he can't go through or around them, he'll go over them (overleaf).

If there was one position in the NFL where new stars were found it was at receiver. Jerry Rice of the 49ers became the number one big-play man in the league, leading the NFC in receptions (86) and touchdowns (15). In the AFC, the Jets' Al Toon emerged as a threat not only receiving but also running after the catch. Toon placed second in conference in catches with 85, pulled down eight TDs and averaged 13.8 each reception. The only one who caught more than Toon and Rice in the league was the Raiders' tight end Todd Christensen. The former BYU-product gathered in an amazing 95 passes. The amazing part was that Christensen played for the quarterback-poor Raiders.

Here are the top receivers:

NFC	Rcpt.	Yds.	Ave.	Tds.
Jerry Rice	86	1,570	18.3	15
Roger Craig	81	624	7.7	0
Ike Smith	80	1,014	12.7	6
Herschel Walker	76	837	11.0	2
Gary Clark	74	1,265	17.1	7
Art Monk	73	1,068	14.6	4
Mark Bavaro	66	1,001	15.2	4
James Lofton	64	840	13.1	4
Charlie Brown	63	918	14.6	4
Dwight Clark	61	794	13.0	2

AFC	Rcpt.	Yds.	Ave.	Tds.
Todd Christensen	95	1,153	12.1	8
Al Toon	85	1,176	13.8	8
Stanley Morgan	84	1,491	17.8	10
Gary Anderson	80	871	10.9	8
Tony Collins	77	684	8.9	5
Matt Bouza	71	830	11.7	5
Steve Largent	70	1,070	15.3	9
Mickey Shuler	69	675	9.8	4
Mark Duper	67	1,313	19.6	11
Billy Brooks	65	1,131	17.4	8

scaffolding. In high school, Rice developed an interest in sport and soon became an outstanding receiver. Colleges called offering scholarships but the one that Rice wanted to attend, Mississippi State, never did. Wanting to stay near his home, Rice settled for Mississippi Valley State, where Archie Cooley, the head coach at the time, used a wide-open offense featuring the receivers. In his final two years in college, Rice put up stunning numbers, catching 214 passes for 3,295 yards. In his senior season Rice scored 28 touchdowns and the pros were in pursuit.

"You'd see him catch 10 in the first half," says New England's player personnel director Dick Steinberg," and you wondered if he could catch 30 a game."

At the NFL scouting combine, where all the professional scouts observe college talent before the draft, Rice was breathtaking. "Jerry was sensational," remembers Paul Hackett, the former San Francisco offensive coordinator who now runs the Dallas offense. "I couldn't believe what I was watching. I couldn't wait to get back to Bill (Walsh) and tell him what I'd seen. And the more we saw, the more we liked. Here was a really good kid with great potential."

So great was Rice's potential that the 49ers traded up with the New England Patriots for the rights to Rice. "We decided to trade up," says Hackett. "We were certain Jerry was the best wide receiver available in the draft and we were almost sure he would last until the middle of the first round."

"I was beside myself," says Rice, remembering the draft day. "My first thought was 'Super Bowl champs, I'm going to get one of those rings for myself.'"

Rice's impact on the 49ers was immediate. His outside speed forced opposing defenses to discontinue double-teaming All Pro Dwight Clark

Phil Simms (right) finally got recognition as an outstanding quarterback by leading the New York Giants to the Super Bowl and completing a record 22 of 25 passes.

on the other side. His acrobatic ability and toughness over the middle was quite apparent.

We played the Raiders in an exhibition game that fall," says Hackett. "Jerry was supposed to run a corner route in the end zone. He went up between three defenders, got bumped, and still came down with the ball. They called him out on the play, but it's still one of the greatest catches I've ever seen. It seemed like he could just hang there in the air forever on that pass, waiting for the ball. I'll never forget it."

Neither will the Raiders. But for Jerry Rice, his career is just starting to take off. Which is good news for the Niners and poison for the rest of the NFL.

Phil Simms

He's not as glamorous as Dan Marino or Jim McMahon. He's not as mobile as Boomer Esiason or Tony Eason. He doesn't have as strong an arm as John Elway or Jay Schroeder. But what Phil Simms does have, more than any of the aforementioned, is guts. Or heart. Or intestinal fortitude. Whatever that extra intangible is, the intangible that makes a man continue in battle, Phil Simms has it. More than any quarterback in the league.

"He's so tough," says Giants wide receiver Phil McConkey. "He's probably the fiercest competitor I've ever met in my life.

"I think I have a pretty good eye for football and a pretty good eye for people," McConkey, a former naval officer, adds. "Let me tell you something about Phil Simms. I've met some POWs, guys who were in camps for six or seven years in Hanoi. God forbid this ever would happen, but if he ever became a POW, he'd be as tough as any of the guys I ever met. He's got guts that just spill out of him. He'd handle it."

Some would say that playing football in New York is almost like being a POW. Phil Simms knows that. So do his teammates. As Lionel Manuel says, "Over the last three years, he's been booed more than any man in the United States, including the president."

Manuel is forgetting about the first five years of Simms' career, when the 6-3, 210 pound Simms was unmercifully booed by Giants fans, fans who didn't believe he could ever lead the team to the Super Bowl. It was so bad, Simms was booed even before he donned a Giants uniform.

Draft day, 1979. The Giants, a team with many holes, none bigger than quarterback, select a kid from Morehead State with the seventh pick of the draft. Sure he's an all-Ohio-Valley Conference second team quarterback, but who ever heard of him. And when the draftniks did hear his name, they booed. And booed. And booed.

To complicate matters, Simms had trouble establishing himself as the quarterback. Injuries dogged him his first few seasons. There was that bruised hand in his rookie campaign. A shoulder separation the following season. Another shoulder separation. Knee surgery during the 1982 preseason. A dislocated thumb the next year. And to top it off, the Giants were bad. Like 3-12-1 bad. Like 4-12 bad. And Simms took the brunt of the fans' frustration.

"When I look back on it now, I didn't come in with a very good team," says Simms. "We were bad and we even got worse. We finally started putting it together after that.

"Players very seldom think the problem is them. I was always the same way. I always thought I was good enough. I know this. For a quarterback to succeed there's got to be some help around him. You've got to be lucky. I mean, for me to complete a pass, I've got to have protection, a guy's got to get open, I've got to throw, he's got to hold it. A lot of things have to happen for me to be good. We had a lot of breakdowns in those days, some of it was my fault, but I know it wasn't all my fault. I knew physically I had a chance to be a pretty good player. I never had my doubts. I really didn't."

He may not have, but others certainly did. And many of the doubters felt that Simms would never play a full season because of his propensity to injuries. Thankfully for Simms and the Giants, one of his biggest boosters is the man who drafted him, general manager George Young.

"The thing that's impressed me the most is that so many times he's had people tell him he's injury-prone," says Young. "That's harder to fight than the pain. It lasts longer than the hurt. He's had to go through that several times. That's a little tougher than a guy recovering from a punch. But Phil Simms is not injury prone, he's accident prone.

"I told Phil, if you ever meet Johnny Unitas, you ought to look at his right hand. His ring finger takes a size 19 ring, the knuckle is so swollen from hitting all those helmets. Unitas took only six steps back. He was a tough guy. And so is Phil. He'll step up. A lot of guys will fade back when they're rushed. Not Unitas. Not Phil."

But the injuries are a thing of the past for Simms. And so are the boos. For the past three seasons, Simms has taken almost 99 percent of the center snaps. With those snaps, he has thrown for more aggregate passing yardage than any quarterback in the league other than Dan Marino. He has proven to be a clutch performer, as evidenced by his fourth and 17 at Minnesota, a pass that was caught by Bobby Johnson and very likely turned the Giants season around.

"He shouldn't be fighting for credibility any more," says Young. "To me, the whole credibility factor is moot. I'm not going to defend this guy any more. He doesn't need it. In one year, he's been MVP of the Pro Bowl and a Super Bowl quarterback.

Perhaps more than anything, Simms' Super Bowl performance squashed any doubts about his talent or ability. Not only did Simms lead the Giants to a Super Bowl victory, but he broke records during a near-flawless display of passing. For the game, Simms hit 22 of 25 passes for 268 yards and three touchdowns. His 88 percent completion rate was the highest in Super Bowl history. Now, Simms doesn't have to take a back seat to anybody. Not Marino. Not Elway. Not anybody.

A triumphant walk. Phil Simms (facing page) never lacked the confidence to make it big in the NFL and in '86 he put it all together. The former number one pick from Morehead State threw for 3,487 yards and 21 touchdowns while leading the Giants to the top.

"I've changed as a quarterback," says Simms. "I do a lot of things better now than I did before. I get rid of the ball fairly quick. I just understand more now than I did when I was younger. Hey, you've just got to learn to be a quarterback in this league."

Simms learned how to win. And the fans have learned how to appreciate a winner.

Al Toon

When he was in college, he dabbled in modern dance, learned to love ballet and took a liking to the ancient martial arts. The most enjoyable sport he participated in was track and field.

Meet Al Toon, star receiver with the New York Jets. Yes, he's a football player. A well-rounded football player. "I don't consider myself a football player," Toon says. "I consider myself an athlete with an ability to be a football player."

As a student at the University of Wisconsin, Toon thought of himself as a track star first, football player second. Not that he wasn't a good football player. He happened to be one of the nation's best. In fact, when he graduated in 1985, Toon left holding almost every receiving record the school has. But as good as he was between the hash marks, he was nearly that good on the track. Toon was a world-class triple jumper, a Big 10 conference champion and talented enough to make the 1984 Olympic trials. He was almost as good in the high jump and high hurdles. With so much athletic talent, is it any surprise that Al Toon emerged in 1986 as one of the most feared receivers in football?

"He has the potential to be one of the greats," says Jets head coach Joe Walton. "There is so much he can do, like catch a ball in a crowd. Guys who can do that usually can't run very fast. But he can make the toughest catch, he can run well enough to make something out of nothing and he can go deep. What else do you want?"

For Walton and the Jets, they'd like Toon to continue along the path he is heading in. Last season, Toon broke all the New York Jets receiving records by catching 86 passes for 1,176 yards. With speedy wide receiver Wesley Walker on his opposite side and young quarterback Ken O'Brien drilling spirals through secondaries, the sky's the limit for this 6-4, 200 pounder.

Prior to draft day in 1985, the Jets had a big decision to make. With the 10th selection in the draft, New York was certainly going to take one of the three blue-chip receivers – Toon, Jerry Rice from Mississippi Valley State, or Eddie Brown from Miami. But which one? New York opted for the all-round athletic ability of Toon. Toon is tall, with an angular frame, large hands and the high jumper's ability. And Jets are not sorry with the choice they made.

"Al can do everything a little man can do, except he's really big," says Jets offensive coordinator Rich Kotite. "The tougher the situation, the more he enjoys it. But he wants to be the best there's been, you see."

The initial relationship between the Jets and Toon was anything but the best. As the 10th player selected in the draft, Toon wanted big bucks to sign a pro contract and he balked at the Jets offers. Toon held out of the entire training camp and the first game of the regular season before New York upped its ante and satisfied the former Badger. Toon started slowly as a pro and was a reserve for all but seven games of his rookie campaign. Those starts, however, were enough to prove his worth. Toon caught 46 passes for 662 yards and his running and jumping ability astounded teammates and opposition alike.

"The most amazing thing is what Al Toon does over the middle," says Jets strong safety Kirk Springs. "That's where you find out a receiver's worth. Al can go up for it, hold on to it, come down with it and run with it. That about covers it."

"You always hear the announcers say that if the guy had broken one tackle, he would have gone 80 yards," says Jets quarterback Ken O'Brien. "The thing is, Al does it."

Like the time against New Orleans when Toon grabbed a ball running across the middle and bounced off five or six Saints before rambling 62 yards for a touchdown. Or the time he took a simple hook pattern against Miami and turned that into a TD. Everytime you looked up in '86, Toon was spiking a ball in the end zone, a credit, Toon says, to a full training camp.

"I'm much better this year for having gone through training camp," Toon says. "Last year I'd run a pattern and stop at the end. I didn't know what to do. Now I'm in control. I have complete awareness of what's going on."

The players trying to defend against Toon always knew what was going on, only they couldn't do anything about it. Toon began '86 in outstanding form and never let up during the season. The result was 86 receptions, over 1,000 yards receiving and respect from every cornerback in the league.

"There are two things you have to be aware of as a receiver," Toon says. "First, you have to get open, which isn't as easy as it sounds. Second, and most important, you have to concentrate on catching the ball. I don't think of where the defender is or where the boundary is – which I think of as another defender, anyway. I just concentrate on catching the ball. But knowing what you're supposed to do and doing it are two different things."

To put it simply, Toon has mastered those two different things. And he has mastered ballet and modern dance and track and field. "I like to be a well-rounded person and everything that has happened to me is helping me grow," says Toon. "I even like football now. And that love is still brewing."

Much to the chagrin of cornerbacks around the NFL.

Curt Warner

At the age of 25, it's hard to imagine that Seattle Seahawks star running back, Curt Warner, is the NFL's Comeback Player of the Year. After all, the former Penn State all-American was the number three selection in the

There is no doubting the ability or intensity of Jets receiver Al Toon (facing page). The second-year man from Wisconsin began dominating defensive backs in '86 as he finished second to Todd Christensen in the AFC in receptions with 85. Seattle's Curt Warner (overleaf) returned to the form that made him NFL rookie of the year in '84 by rushing for over 1,400 yards last season.